# Mel Bay Presents

# DADGA'D ENCYCLOPEDIA

## by Jim Goodin

---

## CD Contents

1. Passage (A Simple Study) [4:01]
2. Fairest Lord Jesus [3:43]
3. The Pretty Girl Milking the Cow [3:53]
4. Si Beag Si Mhor [4:45]
5. Planxty Safaigh [1:56]
6. Quiet Moments [2:40]
7. Moroccan Bluz [2:48]
8. (Floating) About the Clouds [3:43]
9. Quarrel with the Landlady and Standing at the Gate [5:16]
10. Arkansas Traveler [1:53]
11. Farewell to Music [1:47]
12. Hypnosis [3:14]
13. Prelude in G Major [2:38]
14. The Eagle [5:08]
15. Sleep My Wee Child [4:35]

---

1 2 3 4 5 6 7 8 9 0

*Visit us on the Web at www.melbay.com — E-mail us at email@melbay.com*

# DADGAD Encyclopedia

*Scotland - Looking North*

# Opening Thoughts

*Photo by Ann Jeffrey*

Welcome to a collection of music, exercises, scales and ideas designed to introduce you to DADGAD tuning; an open tuning of rich string voicing that will begin a new dimension in your playing. Open tunings can be used on your guitar in addition to standard guitar tuning of EADGBE. Though there is a world of music to be played in standard tuning, open tunings bring immense color and sound to the musical palette. Joni Mitchell and David Crosby are two artists from popular music that feature open tunings prominently in their music. Two artists, whose lives sadly came to an end much too soon, Michael Hedges and Nick Drake, were both tremendous innovators in the use of open tunings in defining their music.

When you listen to many traditional blues players you are hearing open tunings such as open D (DADF♯AD), E (EBEG♯BE) or G (DGDGBD), among others. Though open tunings can be approached with many different techniques including conventional strumming, many guitarists play with fingerstyle technique, bringing out the many colors of the variously tuned strings.

What makes an open tuned guitar richer and more colorful than a guitar in standard tuning are the intervals, meaning the number of musical steps between strings. In several open tunings including this book's focus, DADGAD, there is a configuration of strings that share the same pitches but are an octave apart. Also with DADGAD there is no major 3rd interval as found in standard tuning. In EADGBE a major 3rd between G and B, gives standard tuning its familiar sound. DADGAD takes on a harp-like quality, largely due to the G to B string distance being lowered one whole step on the B string to an A, giving the interval of a major 2nd with an interval of a perfect 4th on both sides of the G and now A strings. This aspect of DADGAD tuning is a key quality that draws many players to it, particularly those playing music with Celtic influence such as Pierre Bensusan and Martin Simpson.

DADGAD was used in the early British folk school and is most credited to folk-guitarist extraordinaire Davey Graham, who composed "Anji." Davey and other players of the time traveled to Morocco, picking up on music and instruments like the Oud. The influence of this period led to using DADGAD on the guitar. One of my pieces in this book, "Moroccan Bluz," was inspired by this influence as well as a desire to write a piece with a 'blues' color.

DADGAD Encyclopedia includes compositions and arrangements ranging in technical level from intermediate fingerstyle to advanced skilled, fusing a blend of techniques including rhythmic strumming, fingerstyle and two-handed tapping. In addition, this book includes scale exercises covering all major and minor keys and chord charts offering familiar, intermediate and advanced chord shapes for those interested in playing rhythmic or strumming style in DADGAD. I've offered thoughts on playing and music that I hope you will find inspiring and encouraging. The book's companion CD, recorded at the studio of composer/guitarist William Ackerman, includes all the compositions and arrangements from the book. I hope you enjoy *DADGAD Encyclopedia* and find it helpful and rewarding in your playing. If you have questions feel free to contact me via email at *jimgoodinmusic@gmail.com* or via postal mail at *Jim Goodin, Wood and Wire Music, 505 9th St., #3L, Brooklyn, NY 11215.*

*Jim Goodin*

# Tuning Techniques - from "standard (EADGBE)" to DADGAD in seconds

Here are several ways to help you adjust your guitar to DADGAD from standard EADGBE tuning. You could use an electronic tuner but I would like to encourage you to gain confidence in tuning by ear. There are times when it is ok to depend on a tuner but it's always been my preference not to. I heard Leo Kottke once say that using an electronic tuner erases your ear and though meant in his rye humorous style, it's always stayed with me.

I'm offering several methods to tune to DADGAD. I encourage you to try each of them and become comfortable using all of them as they can only add to your experience as a guitarist.

## Open String Method

Use the fourth D string as a point of reference and lower the sixth E string as shown in *example 1*, one whole step down to D matching fourth D string an octave lower.

*Example 1. Matching sixth string to fourth string open.*
*(Example 1-6 photos by Ann Jeffrey)*

Now tune the first E string down to D matching your fourth D string one octave higher as in *example 2*.

Only one string now remains in getting your guitar tuned to DADGAD. Lower the second B string one whole step to A, matching the pitch of the fifth A string one octave higher.

Now fret the third G string at the second fret as shown in *example 3* and strum all strings; you'll hear a D chord but with no major or minor 3$^{rd}$ interval. Listen to see if all strings sound in tune. The intervals between the strings low-to-high pitch are fifth, fourth, fifth, unison and fourth so the chord should sound open and full. If any string sounds wavering or out of tune, raise or lower it's tuner to correct it.

*Example 2. Matching first string to fourth string open.*

# Matched Frets Method

Fret the fifth fret on the fifth A string sounding a D. Lower the sixth E string to match it. The sixth string should now be a D one octave lower matching your fretted fifth string.

Fret the second fret on the third G string sounding an A. Lower second B string to match the pitch of the fretted A. Fret the fifth fret on the second B string now tuned to an A, sounding a D. Lower the first E string one whole step to D to match.

Again fret the second fret of the third G string as shown in *example 3* and strum all strings, listening to hear that their perfect fifth, fourth and unison intervals ring in tune with the familiar D chord.

*Example 3: Playing D chord to check tuning*

## Tuning by Harmonics

As in the *open-string method* begin by tuning the sixth E string down a whole step to match the fourth D string open. Play a seventh fret harmonic on the fourth D string sounding an A as shown in *example 4* and lower the second B string one whole step down to match it. If the harmonic technique is new to you, see my section on *Playing Harmonics – Natural and Artificial* later in the book.

*Example 4. Matching the second string open to the seventh fret harmonic on the fourth D string.*

Play a harmonic at the seventh fret on the third G string as shown in *example 5*, and lower the first E string one whole step to a D to match it.

*Example 5. Matching the first string open to the seventh fret harmonic on the third G string.*

As before, to check the tuning of all the strings (at the second fret on the third G fret an A string) as shown in *example 6* and strum all strings. Listen for the clear open fifth, fourth and unison intervals to hear that the strings are in tune.

*Example 6. Playing D chord to check tuning.*

*Performing with Language of 3, Blah Blah Lounge, Brooklyn, NY.*
*Photo by Matt Richards.*

If you successfully blend fingerpicking American folk blues with Celtic melodies and Indian raga improvisation, you've got Jim Goodin. He is playing out of so many sources that he sounds exactly like himself. He produces a flowing river of sound that you can listen to straight through or dip in and out of as you write, paint or create new ideas. The best recommendation for his music is all the people who come up to me when I play his music at my school: "Who is that playing – I feel so good hearing it." I've owned his CD, *Celtic Journey to the Path* since its first edition, and its synthesis of originality and timelessness keeps it new and pleasing. – *Richard Schaub, Ph.D*

# Familiar Chords in DADGAD

It's possible some of you working through this book may be more accustomed to playing the guitar in a chord strumming style or you may be looking for chord shapes in DADGAD to accompany your voice or other instruments. I will provide a few sections of chords, beginning with familiar ones that many of us learned in our early guitar lessons. Later in the book you'll find chord shapes for Major and Minor 7th's as well as a section with more colorful chords such as minor 6/9 and major and minor 9th chords often used in the jazz guitar style.

The chords for the I-IV-V progressions of the major keys C, D, E and F are shown in this section. Many folk, country and rock songs follow this kind of chord structure. In the key of C, the chords are C, the 'I' chord built on the first note of the C scale, F, the 'IV' chord built on the fourth note of the scale, and G, the 'V' chord, built on the fifth note of the scale.

In every example I provide three different positions on the fretboard for each chord. The initial focus is on the first seven frets while later in the book the more advanced shapes will be offered up to the twelfth fret.

In each chord diagram all strings are intended to be strummed unless there is an (X) on that particular string, meaning to mute or not play that string.

*Guitar detail*

C major    C major    C major    F major    F major    F major

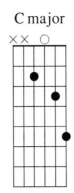 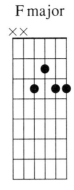 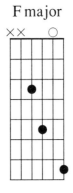 

G major    G major    G major

○ = play open
✕ = not played
⌒ = barre
T = Thumb

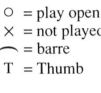 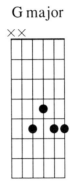 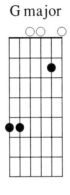 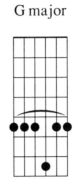

D major    D major    D major    G major    G major    G major

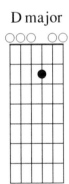 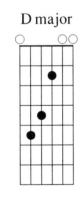 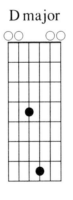 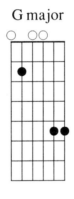 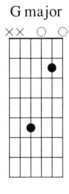 

A major    A major    A major

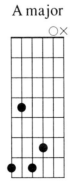 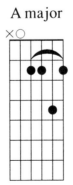

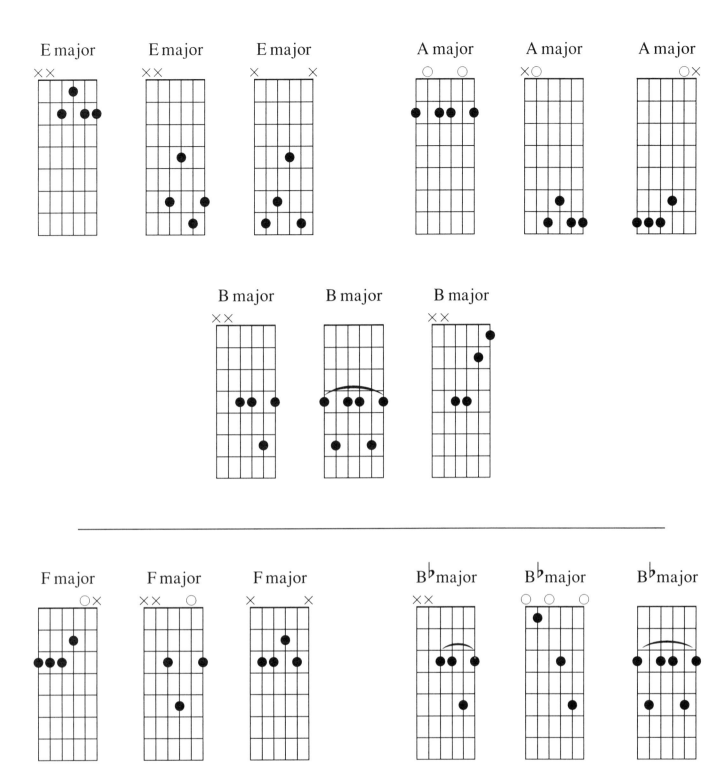

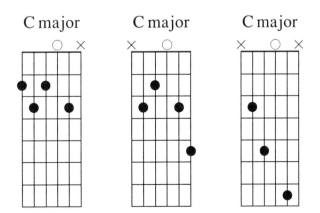

"His original compositions subtly recall influences such as Will Ackerman and Ralph Towner, but Goodin is no copycat, finding his own personal harmonic 'space' in the context of a solo guitar recording." - *Guitar9 Records*

*An early CD demo cover, Jim and son Jamie, age 2.*

# Evolving the Fretboard I - The Majors

One of the best ways to build your playing confidence and technique across the entire guitar fretboard is through scale exercises. The great thing about the guitar's design is how its relationship to note position and open strings works very symmetrically. For example in standard tuning the E on the fourth string at the second fret can be played on the fifth string at the seventh fret as well as at the twelfth fret on the sixth E string. The core chord positions we learn as beginning guitarists can equally be found at other neck locations giving different sound and color. The more you as a guitarist learn about the complete fretboard the more in control of your music and instrument you'll become.

This section, *Evolving the Fretboard I – The Majors* is a start to building confidence and instrument knowledge. This series of scale exercises begins with a D major scale and ascends chromatically through the G major scale. Later in the book we'll address the remaining major scales. Where possible, I have shown each scale in three octaves. The goal is to help you become more comfortable moving about the entire fretboard of the guitar and to think globally as opposed to fixed note or chord positions. I want you to envision the instrument as a whole.

Every scale exercise in each of these sections makes use of a technique I learned years ago from a Chet Atkins column in *Frets* magazine. His concept was to use an open string as a pivot point to move from one note position to another and to extend that technique to be able to play the same notes in multiple locations. For example with a D major scale in DADGAD you begin with open D on the sixth string, then E at the second fret, F-sharp at the fourth and G at the fifth. Play the A open on the fifth string, then shift to the ninth fret on the sixth D string to play the B. Play the C-sharp at the eleventh and then shift to play the open D on the fourth string. With each scale the tablature is mapped out with this technique where possible. The pivot point idea works wonderfully in DADGAD as it does in standard tuning.

Play these exercises slowly at first while you are discovering the location of the notes on the fretboard. Though scales generally have speed built into them the more familiar you get with the pattern, this is not the point. I want you to watch and learn how to move about the fretboard and discover how you can play almost any one note in several different places on the instrument.

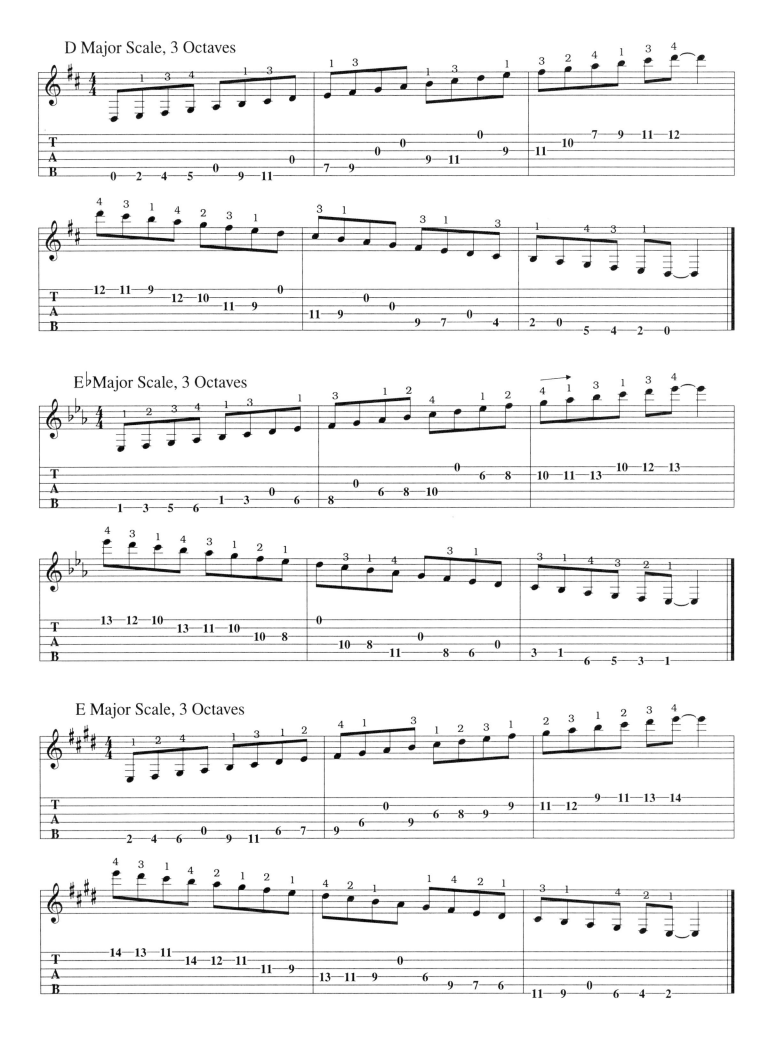

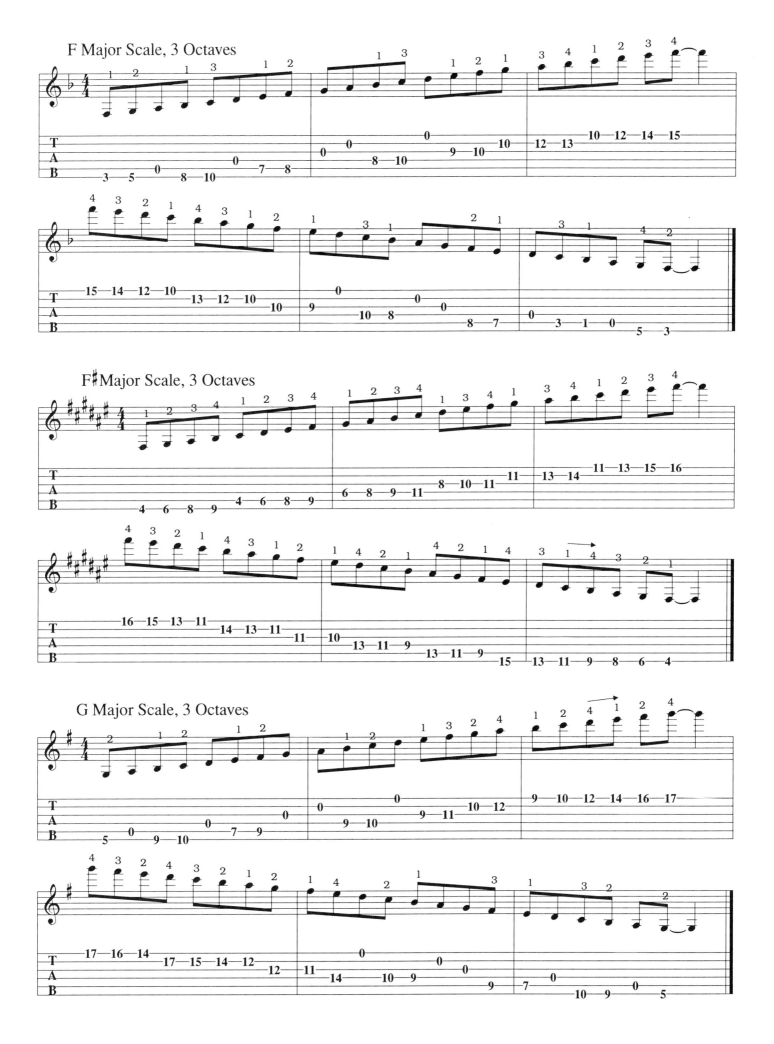

*Through the Door, illustration by Paul Bianca*

# Passage (A Simple Study)

Here's a piece that you could easily play even if never exposed to DADGAD tuning and one that works with the sound of the tuning. *Passage* is based upon a chordal D major scale covering three octaves and most of the guitar's neck. The piece is essentially arpeggios so you can clearly hear the sound of the open string intervals as the bass part changes chordally in the opening measures and the treble strings change much the same from letter B-D.

The opening measures through letter B are based on a D major scale going up the neck one octave and back down. Bar the three low strings with the first finger from measure 2 up to measure 14. At measure 7 change to your first three fingers for fretting the C-sharp, G and C-sharp, where the pattern briefly changes. Resume the three-string bar for the descending measures that follow.

Letters B-D are each based on a D major scale going down three octaves. These sections make use of a pull-off from the stopped note to the open D string.

When I recorded this piece I subconsciously varied the repeats of the second section so the song form goes AABBBABB. Musically it seemed to work so I chose not to edit.

*Passage (A Simple Study)* can be performed slowly or moderately fast, but should be played with feeling.

*Photo by Corin Nelsen*

# Passage
## (A Simple Study)

Jim Goodin (BMI)

*Slowly, Flowing*

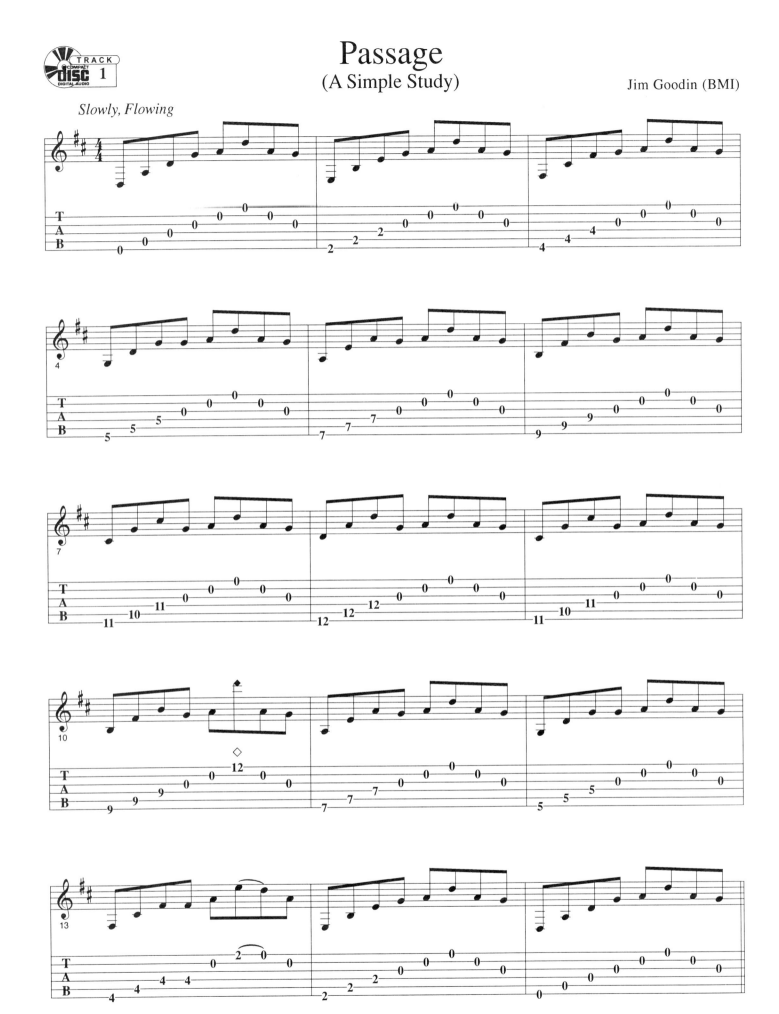

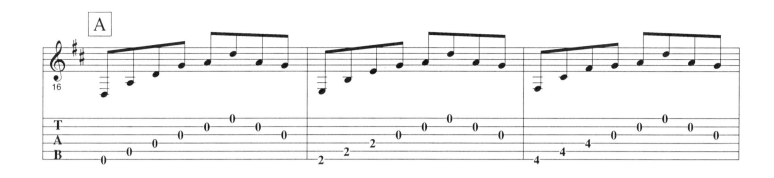

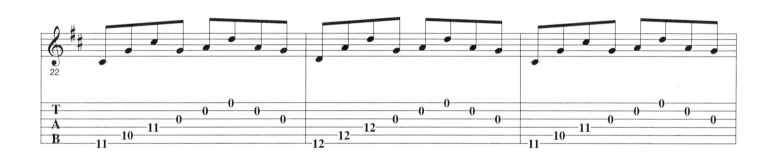

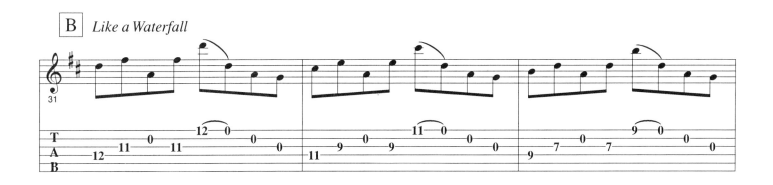

B *Like a Waterfall*

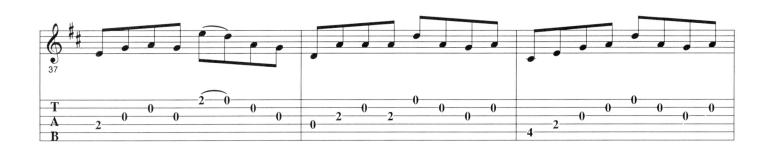

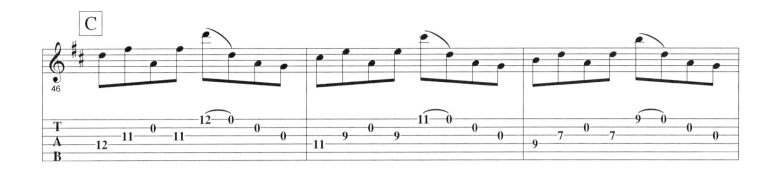

E

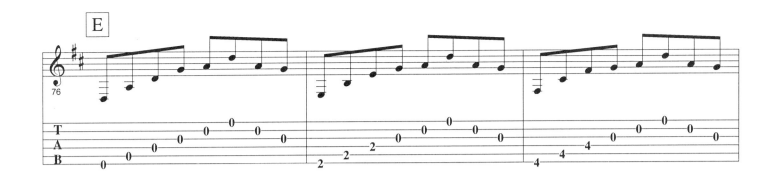

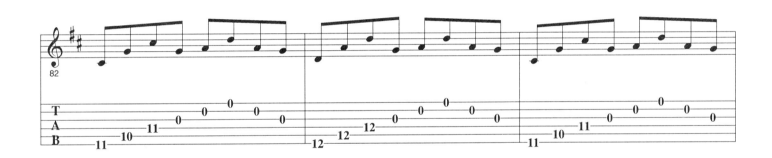

23

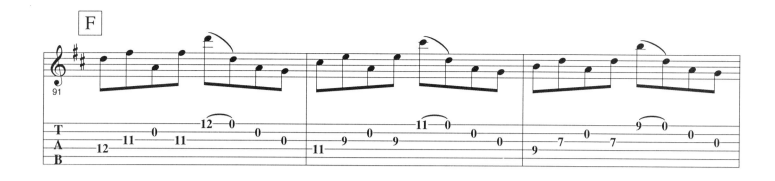

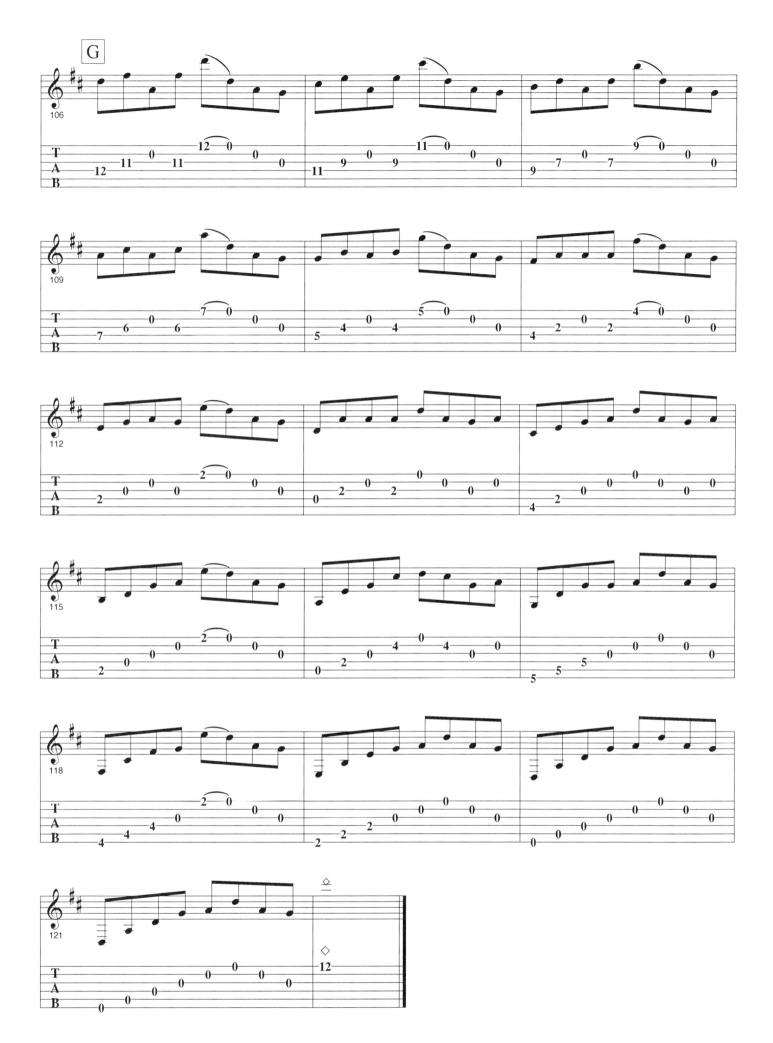

*"the most moving and melodic guitar playing in recent memory"*
**Sam Ash® music**

*"a master technician"* **Gig® magazine**

You don't realize its power at first. It creeps up on you like a rolling fog on a starless night revealing itself only under the brilliant glow of a midsummer's moon. The subtle complexity of the music woven by acoustic guitar master Jim Goodin lulls you, draws you in and welcomes you to a comfortable, secluded spot. While a sharp ear may spot Ralph Towner's and Michael Hedges' influences in Goodin's elegant fingerstyle techniques and inspired harmonic textures, reducing Goodin to a simple clone doesn't do him or his music justice. Make no mistake: Goodin's acoustic creations have zest, zeal and originality. Goodin's blend of acoustic Celtic/New Age/world music showcases a percussive attack rife with pull-offs, tantalizing tapping and multi-layered, multi-cultural musical voicings.

*Excerpt from Internet biography by Will Romano*

*Jim Goodin (3rd from left) in performance with (left to right) Raed El-Khazen, Ray Istorico and Will Romano.*
*Brooklyn 7th Heaven Street Fair. Photo by Sharon Romano*

# Fairest Lord Jesus

I experimented with arranging this beautiful old hymn many years ago and left it unfinished. I came across a snippet of the arrangement as I did research for this book. I originally started arranging it in another tuning used by guitarist El McMeen, CGDGAD, but started playing my sketch and found it played well in DADGAD so I chose to bring it to this book's collection.

The opening measures are to be played very stately and church like; then at letter A more reflective.

With measure 15, the arrangement moves to an interlude pattern using harmonics and arpeggios to contrast the chord-like opening.

Looking back, the inspiration for this arrangement came from pieces I used to listen to by the legendary John Fahey, like his arrangement of *In Christ There Is No East or West*.

# Fairest Lord Jesus

Traditional
Arranged by Jim Goodin (BMI)

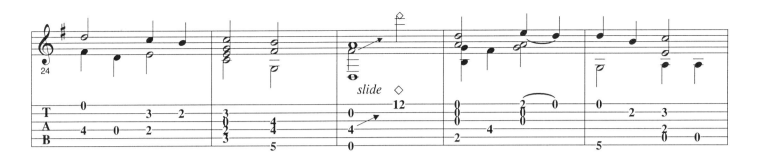

*Freely But With Groove*

29

*Less Stately*

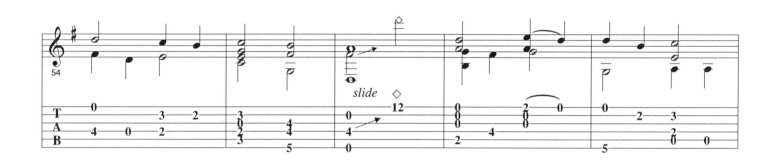

*Freely But With Groove*

# The Pretty Girl Milking the Cow

I first became aware of this tune from an interpretation by guitarist, Stefan Grossman. I believe he did it in dropped-D (DADGBE). I've never been able to discover the tune's composer. Some have credited it to O'Carolan but most transcriptions show it as Irish traditional.

This arrangement is straightforward divided into repeated "A" and "B" sections. The "A" sections are centered in A minor and "B" shifts to the relative major key of C.

The feeling should be of color and expression with a vision of the beautiful country the song was written about, fading with the harmonic section at the end.

*Vermont - Pastoral River and hills*

# Pretty Girl Milking the Cow

Traditional
Arranged by Jim Goodin (BMI)

*Flowing Pastorial*

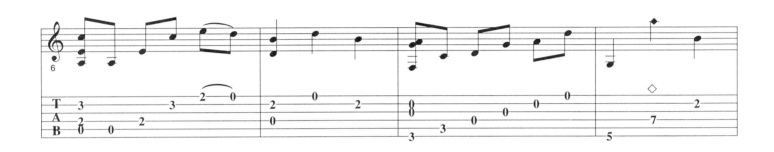

*a tempo*

C

D

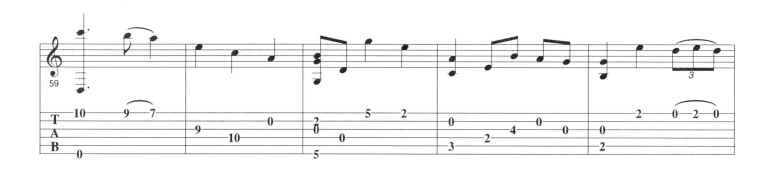

E

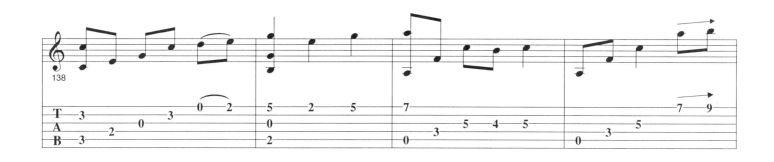

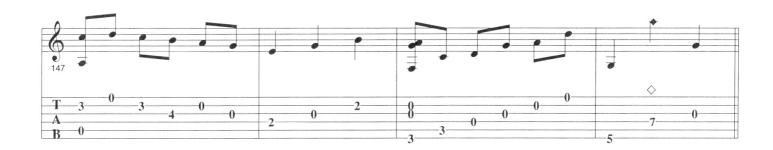

J

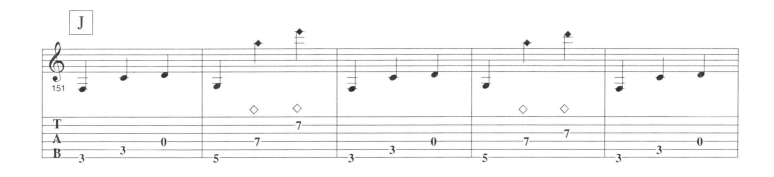

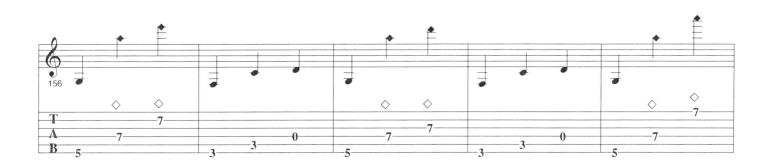

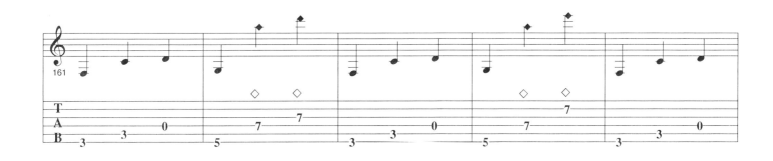

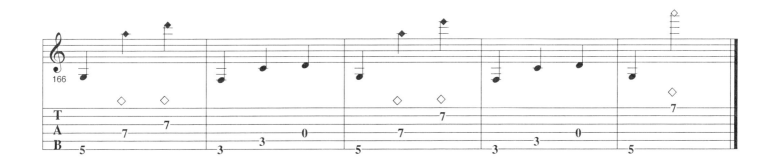

# Who Was Turlough O'Carolan?

Turlough O'Carolan was known as the musical patron saint of Ireland. Living from 1670 to 1738, he was a harpist and has been called Ireland's greatest composer. He traveled throughout his native country as an itinerant folk harpist composing tunes for almost everyone he met.

The amazing thing about this man was that for all of his musical life he was blind, having been stricken by polio in his late teens. A family friend whom he would later commemorate in song, Mrs. Elizabeth McDermott Roe of Ballyfarnon, gave the youthful Turlough his first harp and the opportunity to study, and so determined his destiny.

There are many accounts of his life as a harpist. One collection says that he was not known as a great player of the harp but was one day playing for a patron who suggested that he might make better use of his tongue than fingers, advising that he should become a songwriter. It turned out to be his mission statement, as he would thereafter compose his most popular song, one that has been interpreted by hundreds of modern musicians. I'm speaking of *Si Beag Si Mhor*, translated from Gaelic as "the little hill" and "the big hill." Historical accounts tell us that this tune was about two groups of warring fairies in old Ireland. My arrangement follows.

O'Carolan melodies can be of simple folk quality as in *Si Beag,* but can also be technically demanding, showing influence from the classical contemporaries whom Turlough clearly admired. One tune exhibiting this quality is O'Carolan's *Quarrel with the Landlady*, also included in this collection. Of his some 200 compositions handed down, O'Carolan left us with a final stirring piece, composed shortly before his death, *Farewell to Music*, which comes later in the book.

# Si Beag Si Mhor

O'Carolan was said to have been visiting a friend when he composed this charming melody. The story tells that he wrote this tune while looking out on the pastoral fields and hills behind the house and either saw or imagined two groups of fairies fighting over the territory.

This melody is open to a range of interpretation and has been recorded so frequently that I refer to it as "O'Carolan's greatest hit"! It plays well in DADGAD and particularly in the key of D although, after you learn the tune, you might want to experiment with it in other keys. I play another version in the key of C with the guitar tuned DADGCE.

*Si Beag* is in two song sections. In this arrangement I've laid it out four times, the first staying true to the melody and the others, beginning with the second statement, fusing more harmony. Once through the four sequences the arrangement repeats in its entirety.

Play it freely with feeling. Listen to the recording for the feel. I play it very dreamy, which is the way I think O'Carolan composed it, with emotion and feeling and less attention to strictness of tempo.

# Si Beag Si Mor

Turlough O'Carolan
Arranged by Jim Goodin (BMI)

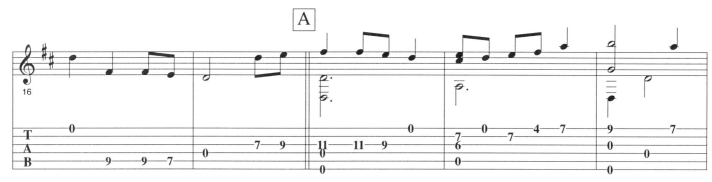

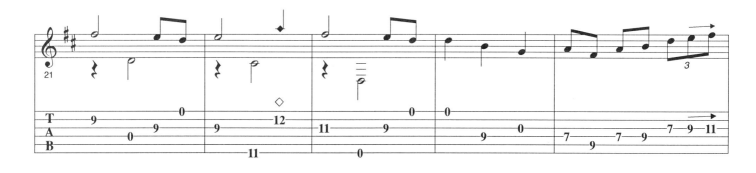

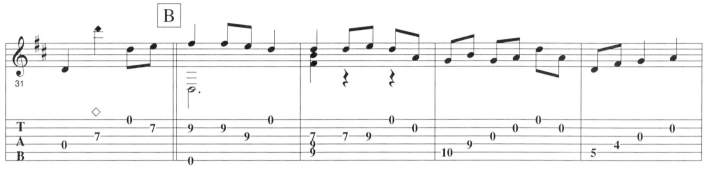

46

E | *slight increase in tempo*

*back to lyrical tempo*

# DADGAD Short – Thinking of O'Carolan

In this *DADGAD Short* I began thinking of a linear exercise to play using the pivot principle that I've spoken of often in the book, that is using open strings to move to different locations on the fretboard. I then harmonized the melody line and came up with what brings to mind the feeling of an O'Carolan flavored tune.

Jim Goodin (BMI)

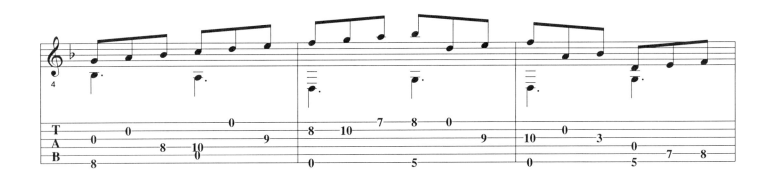

# Planxty Safaigh

*Guitar Detail*

I first learned this great O'Carolan tune from a book by Celtic harpist Sylvia Woods. It reminds me of the flavor of Bach and Corelli, who were both influences.

Pay careful attention to my tablature in measures 17-21 and the repeated measures in 27-30, 53-56 and 63-66, to get the most color from the ringing strings. Play it with pep and zest similar to the feel of Bach's *Bourée in E minor.*

# Planxty Safaigh

Turlough O' Carolan
Arranged by Jim Goodin (BMI)

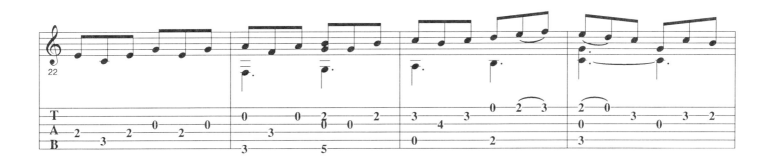

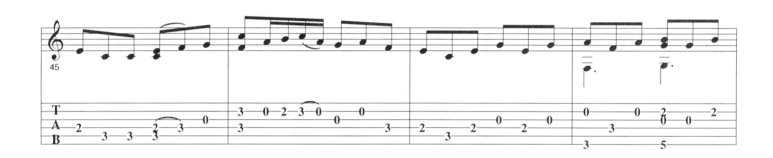

# Chords of Change, Chords of Growth

This collection of chords continues with the format presented earlier in the book with each chord being shown in a I-IV-V chord cycle for the given key. The keys include E-flat major, D minor, E minor, F minor, F-sharp minor and G minor.

These chords cover the first seven frets of the fretboard with three variations provided for each chord. My purpose in doing this is to continue to encourage the thought of fretboard movement and help you break from familiar positions that you have retained from standard tuning and may be looking for in DADGAD. There is nothing wrong with having places to start, but the more you know your way around the guitar fretboard, the more free and confident you will feel in your playing.

*My youngest audience – daughter Callie's first grade class.*

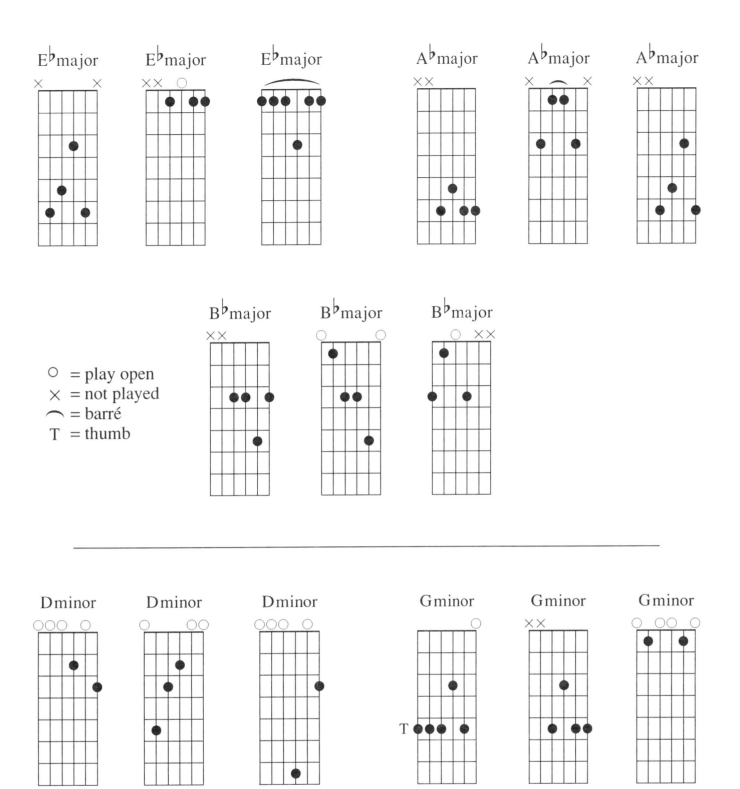

○ = play open
✕ = not played
⌢ = barré
T = thumb

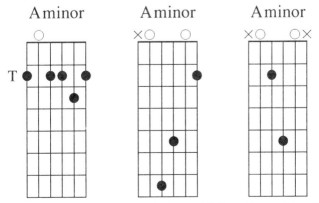

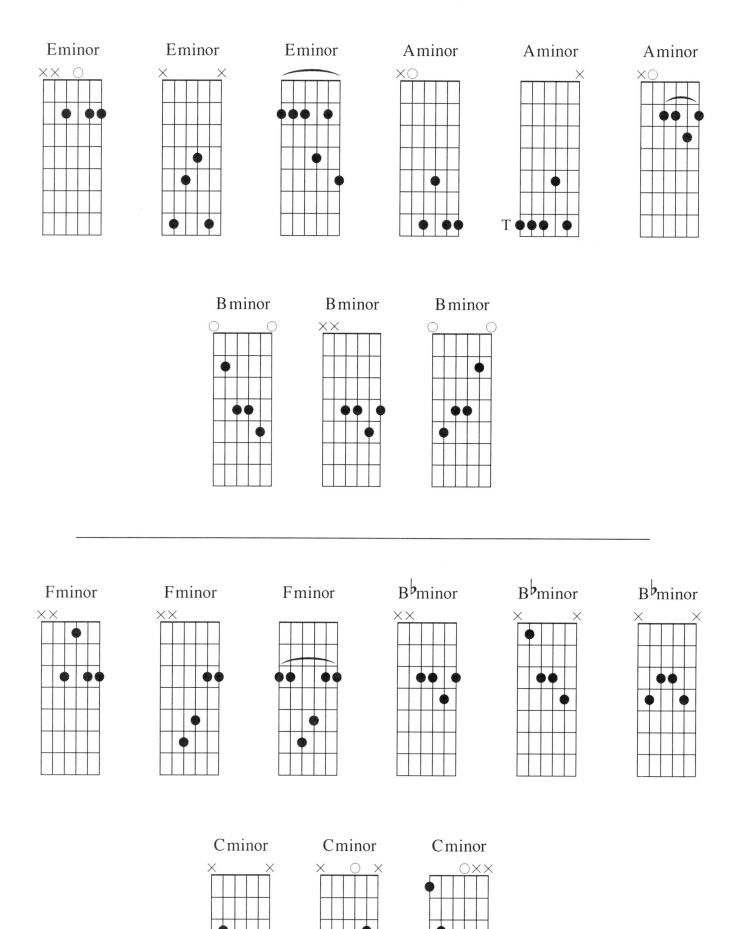

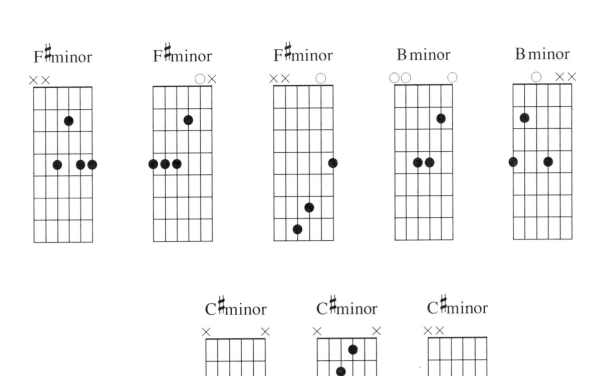

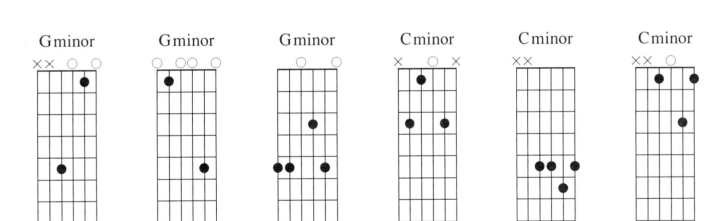

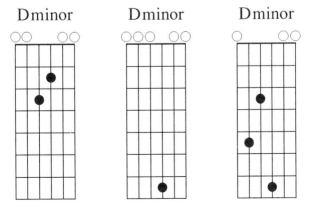

# Evolving the Fretboard II – The Minors

Like the major scale exercises earlier in the book, part of the continuing evolution of your knowledge of the guitar fretboard includes working with the minor keys. Here is a collection of scales focusing on the minors. Minor keys are relatives to major keys but their range is a minor 3rd interval down from the major key. For example C major's relative minor key is A minor. Its A minor scale would begin on A and all twelve notes would be natural pitches meaning no alteration of notes with a sharp or flat.

With minor scales there are three modes for each key. They are the natural, harmonic and melodic minor scales. The natural minor scale as mentioned above has only its relative pitches to its major key as the C major and A minor example. In the A minor harmonic scale mode the 7th scale note, G, is raised a half step or sharped in pitch, making it a G-sharp. This is done in every natural minor key to create the harmonic minor scale equivalent. The raised 7th degree occurs on both the ascent and descent of the harmonic minor scale.

The melodic minor mode raises the sixth *and* seventh notes a half step going up the scale; coming down, the altered notes are lowered to their natural pitches. So with the A minor example, the notes going up are A, B, C, D, E, F-sharp, G-sharp and A. Coming down the pitches would be A, G-natural, F-natural, E, D, C, B and A.

In this section I begin with D minor and ascend chromatically to G minor, covering all three modes mentioned above for each scale.

As with the major scale examples, I have presented the minor scales in three octaves where possible. They also use the pivot note technique meaning that certain notes are to be played on an open string allowing you to shift note positions. In DADGAD this technique works beautifully and will develop your confidence in moving easily about the guitar fretboard.

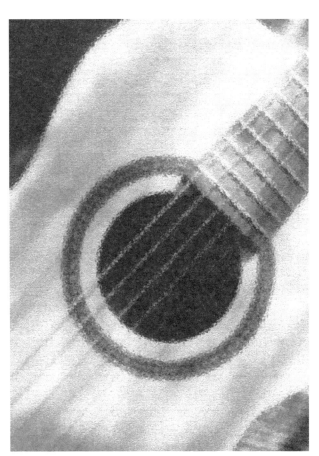

*Guitar detail*

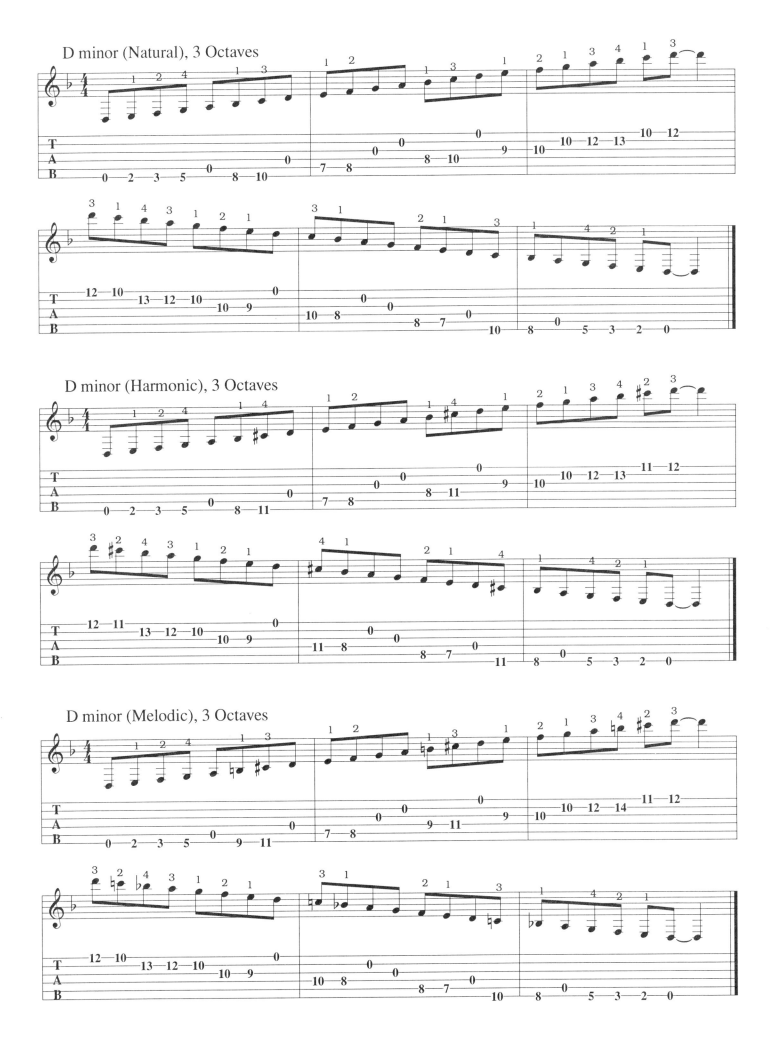

D minor (Natural), 3 Octaves

D minor (Harmonic), 3 Octaves

D minor (Melodic), 3 Octaves

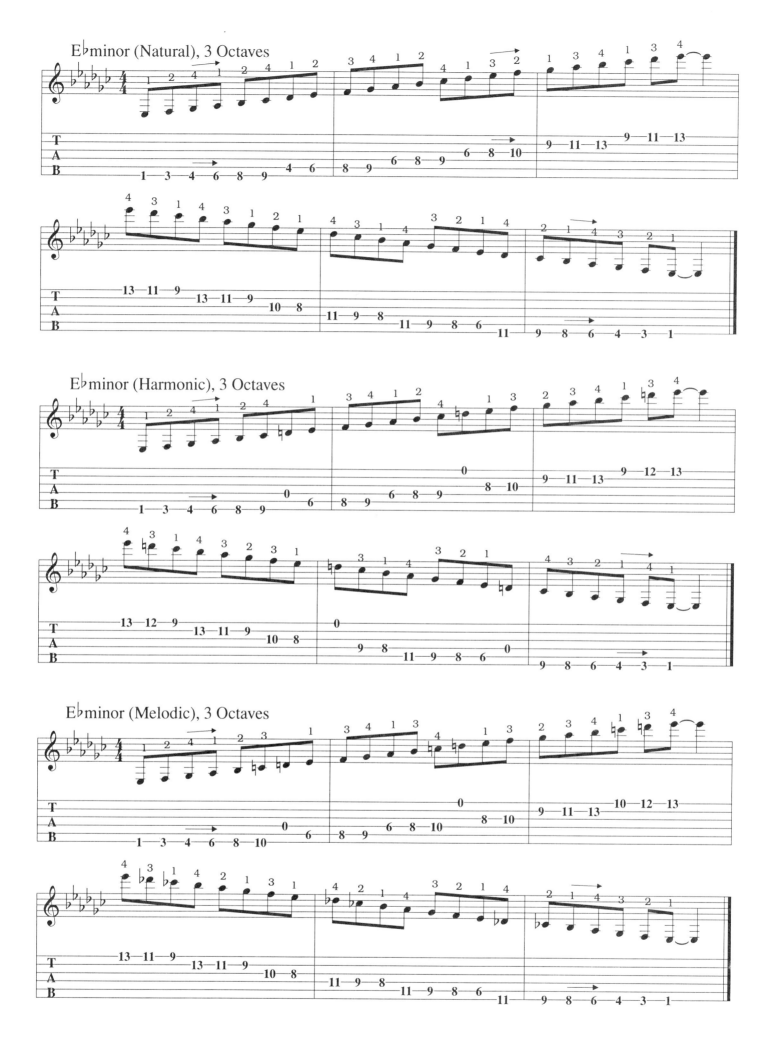

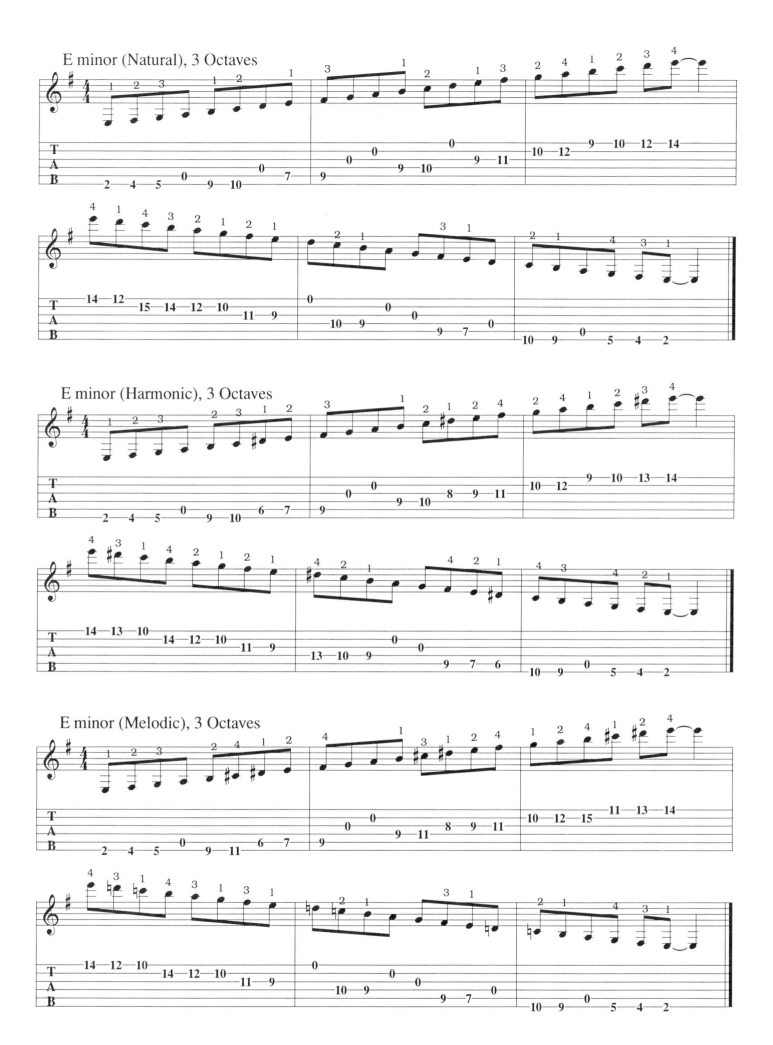

E minor (Natural), 3 Octaves

E minor (Harmonic), 3 Octaves

E minor (Melodic), 3 Octaves

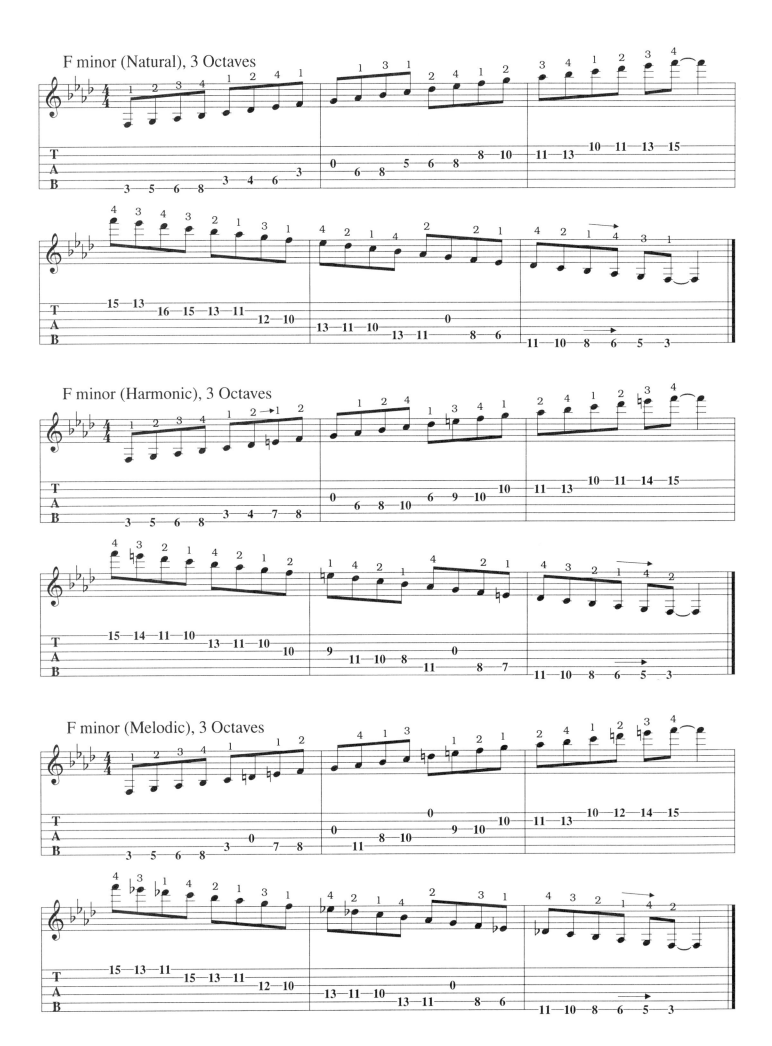

F minor (Natural), 3 Octaves

F minor (Harmonic), 3 Octaves

F minor (Melodic), 3 Octaves

66

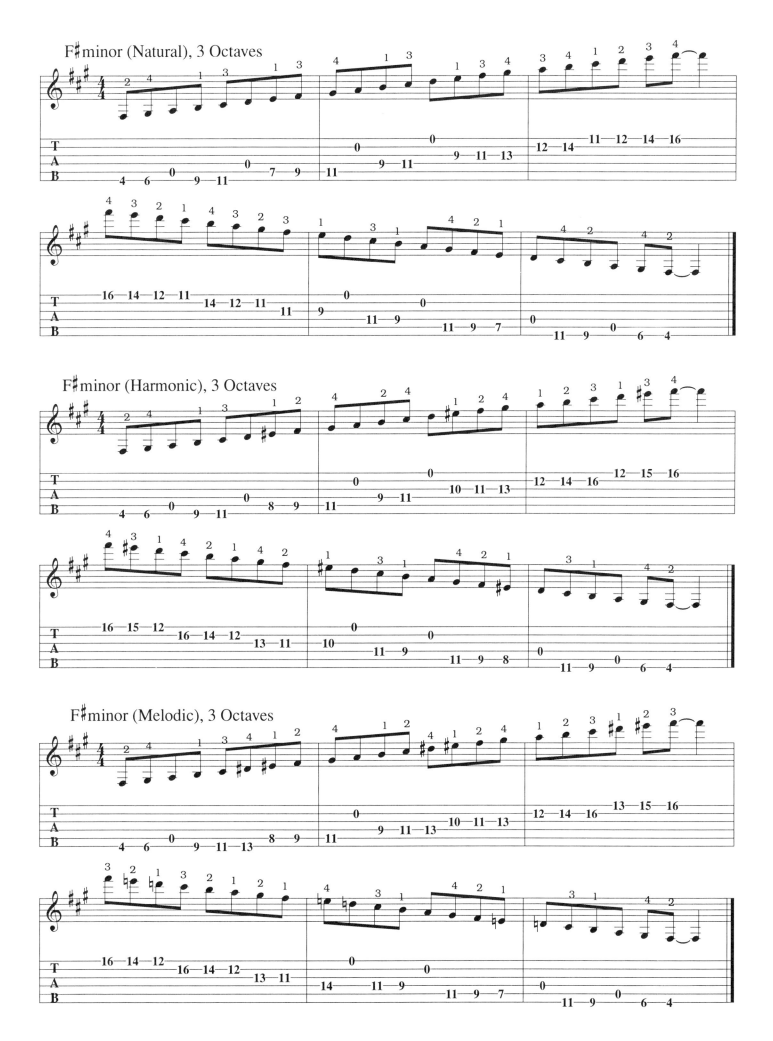

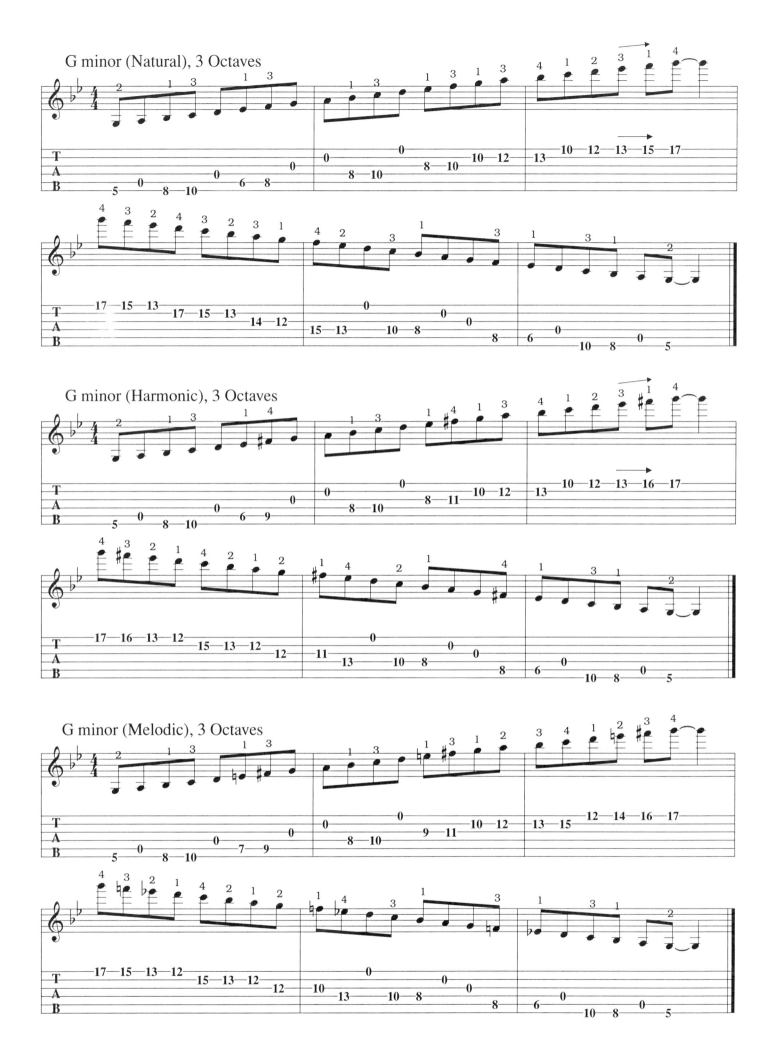

G minor (Natural), 3 Octaves

G minor (Harmonic), 3 Octaves

G minor (Melodic), 3 Octaves

# Quiet Moments

I composed this song inspired by "Si Beag Si Mhor" and sometimes perform it as a segue from *Si Beag*. I recorded the pair together on my CD, *Celtic Journey to the Path*. "Quiet Moments" contrasts between colors of prettiness and dissonance, indicative of much of my writing. I am also a photographer and studied rather seriously at one time, delving into the concept of the *zone system* established by photographer *Ansel Adams*. Adams set up a concept in photographing whereby the picture was divided into sections of light-to-dark for exploring the nuances as well as the contrast of the image. Undoubtedly that influence has had a bearing on my music.

Play "Quiet Moments" with the feeling of sneaking in very quietly at the beginning and allow the piece to build as you play it.

"Quiet Moments" closes with a glimmer of the opening melody of O'Carolan's *Si Beag*.

*Baileys Island, Maine*

# Quiet Moments

*Reflective, pretty, open feeling*

Jim Goodin (BMI)

# Moroccan Bluz

When I first received the offer to do this book I was asked to contribute a blues tune in DADGAD. I composed "Moroccan Bluz" with that in mind and though this tune is not the traditional 12-bar blues, I tried to communicate a blues quality.

In measure 38 and the bars that follow, play the bass note on the sixth D string and then do a muted strum of the notes as shown in notation and tablature. This strum occurs at other places noted in the arrangement.

According to the British folk school, DADGAD tuning was influenced by the Moroccan instrument, the oud, which uses a variation of this tuning, so "Moroccan Bluz" isn't such a stretch after all. The piece begins with a stride piano feel in the base line then moves to more harmonic color indicative of jazz flavoring.

Play this tune with a bit of bounce and fun.

*Tracking "Moroccan Bluz" at Imaginary Road Studios. Photo by Corin Nelsen*

# Moroccan Bluz

Jim Goodin (BMI)

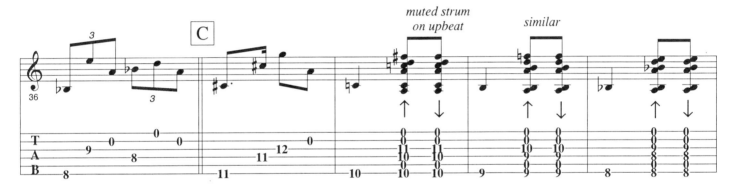

79

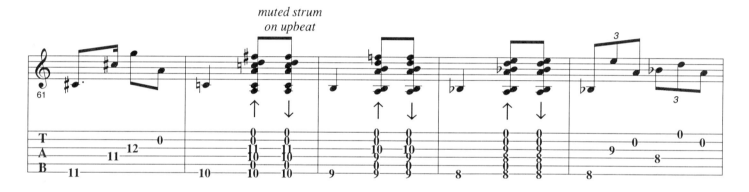

E

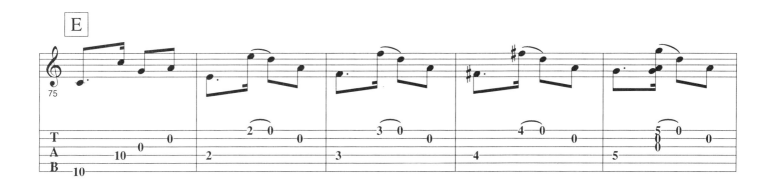

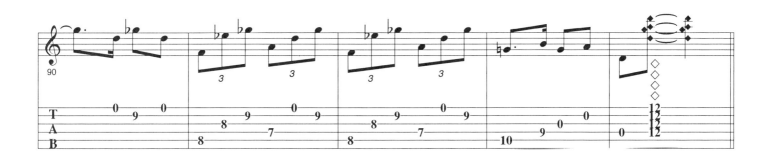

F

*Guitarist/tape loop artist Daryl Shawn (left) and Jim Goodin in the first 'live, in person' performance of their acoustic guitar looping duo Chinapainting, at the Center for Improvised Music, Brooklyn, NY. Photo by Lucio Westmoreland/Jamie Goodin.*

# Thoughts on Music and Seeking Your Voice

The guitar and the expression of music are truly wonderful invitations and experiences that each of us has had the good fortune to encounter. Everybody comes to the instrument in their own way and the approach, regardless of who gave you your first instruction or lesson, becomes very personally defined the more you discover, experience and grow as a musician; therein lays the magic of finding your own voice.

I don't believe in a predetermined "natural talent" that some are and others not, given or that he or she simply has music. I believe we all do. The spirituality of music staying with us is to me a matter of how the early inception whether it was when we were kids or later as adults, was and is nurtured and encouraged. I had the good fortune of being exposed to music including the guitar and other instruments at several intervals in my childhood and adolescent years and for that I'm forever grateful. The real focus and love that I share for the guitar and music really, didn't completely come into play until my mid-20's. Though there were periods of work and learning that came before, it wasn't until I heard the late Michael Hedges in the early 80s that I suddenly realized the defining of my voice as a musician and guitarist. It wasn't so much the guitar technique, ideas or even as Michael would call it, "guitarawarness", as it was a true sense of musical focus and identity that I gained and became aware of through the exposure to him. Regardless of one's choice of instrument, I believe the keys are simply those two elements, focus and identity.

*Frenchman's Bay, Maine.*

# (Floating) About the Clouds

I composed *(Floating) About the Clouds* (originally titled *Floaters*) while living in my native state of Arkansas. When I moved to New York, I had the pleasure of studying with Frederick Hand, the renowned classical guitarist, teacher and *Mel Bay* author. I studied composition with him and greatly expanded this piece while working with him. I dedicate the spirit of that time and this piece to him.

In the beginning play the harmonic measures very lightly as if bouncing from one cloud to another if we could do that. There are two distinct melodies in this composition, with the second beginning at letter C acting as a call-and-response to the first at letter A.

This composition is one of several that grew out of influence of Michael Hedges and some of his wonderful pieces like "Two Days Old," "The Magic Farmer" and "Lenono." See my *Suggested Listening* section later in the book for recommended recordings by Michael and other artists.

# (Floating) About the Clouds

Jim Goodin (BMI)

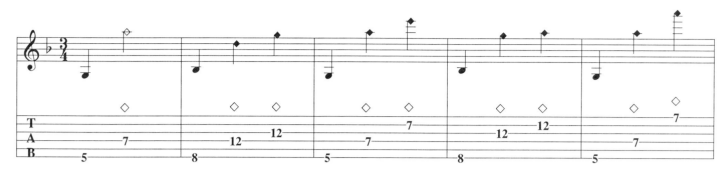

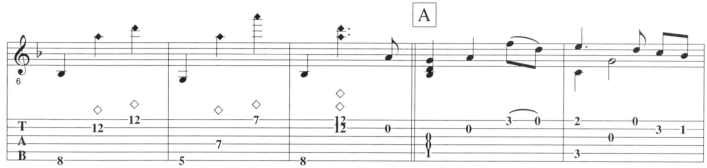

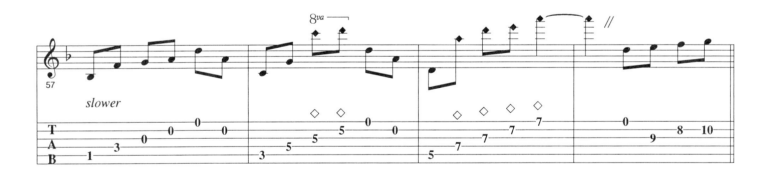

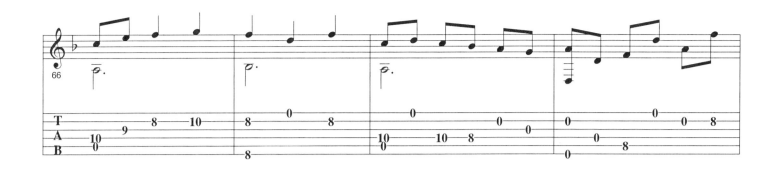

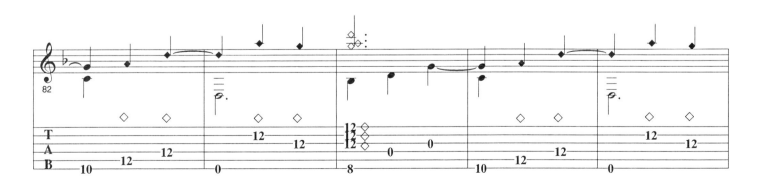

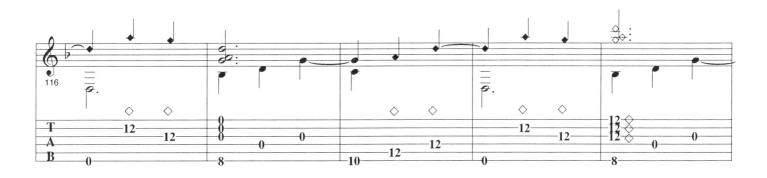

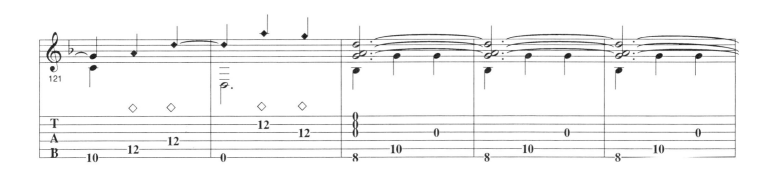

# For Blues, for Jazz and I-IV-V

This section of DADGAD chords will show you the effect of the addition of the seventh to the V chord. Our previous examples have been triads consisting of the root, third and fifth. When you add another third interval on top of the fifth, for example in a C major chord we have, C the root, E the third, G the fifth and now the B seventh-chord. This spelling is for a C major $7^{th}$ chord. Major $7^{th}$ chords are sometimes called "pretty chords", due to a sense of color suggested by the major seventh interval between the root and seventh. This dissonance combined with a third or third and fifth in the chord gives it the "pretty" quality.

The flatted or dominant $7^{th}$ chord is often used in blues. The spelling for this chord is C, E, G and B-flat. In many of our song cadences in blues and rock music, I-IV-$V^7$ progressions have become standard. In the I-IV-$V^7$ progression in the key of C, the $G^7$ chord is spelled G-B-D-F.

For a minor seventh chord spelling we would have C, E flat, G and B-flat spelling a C minor $7^{th}$. An often used chord cadence utilizing minor sevenths is ii-$V^7$-I, or $Dm^7$ $G^7$-C to complete our C major example. Adding a $Cmaj^7$ to the end would give a nice colorful sound. This cadence is familiar in jazz.

As with the previous examples this section includes three position variations for each chord within the first 7 frets of the guitar fretboard. Instead of showing this section in I-IV-V chord cycles I have shown these chords in sequence of a minor seventh, seventh and major seventh on each page. The reasoning for this is that though not strictly limited to being used as the V chord in the I-IV-V cycle, it gives a sense of resolution to the I chord. Though the II minor seventh – V seventh – I would be different, I've felt it more useful to focus this section showing each chord in sequence with its family of sevenths. The chords covered are G, E, F, D, C, A, B, E-flat, B-flat and A-flat.

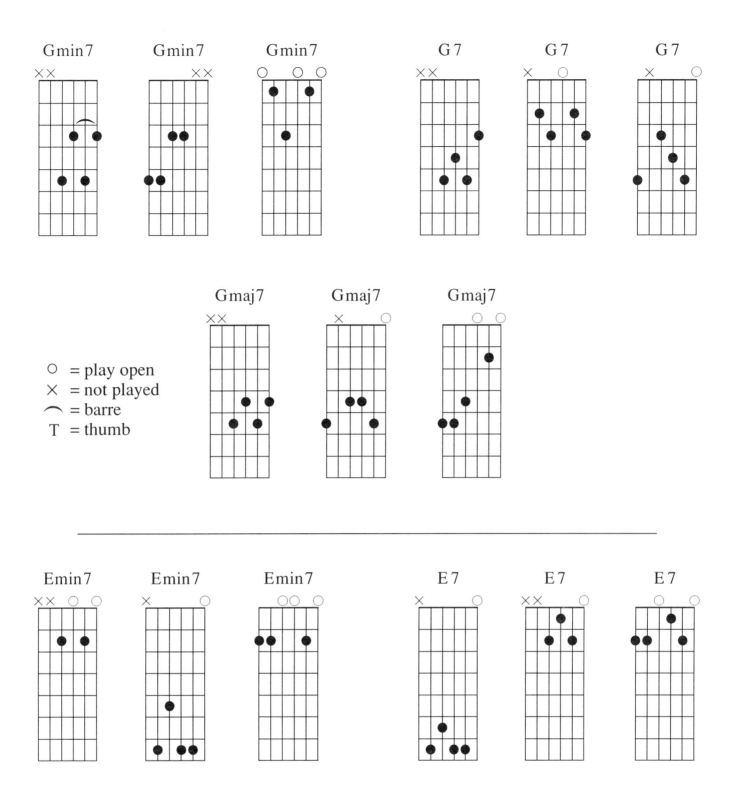

O = play open
X = not played
⌒ = barre
T = thumb

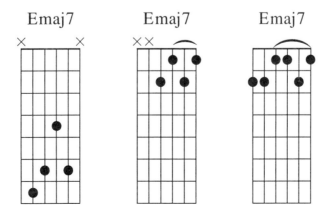

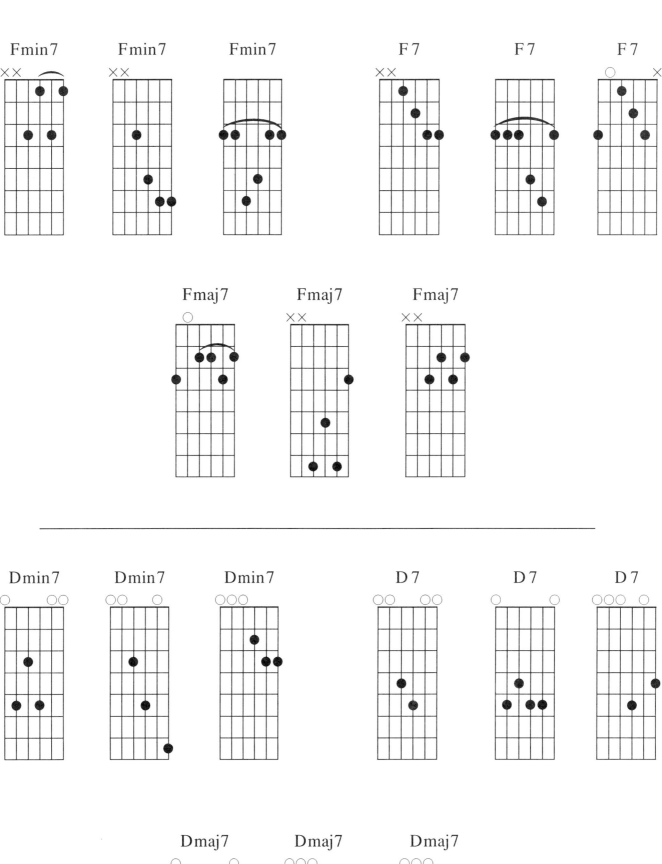

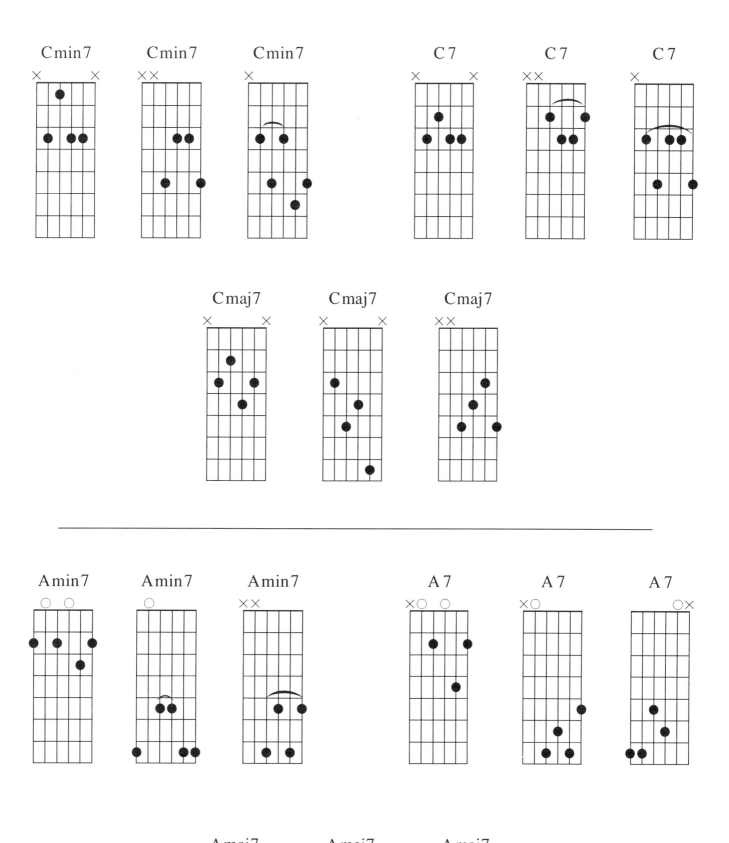

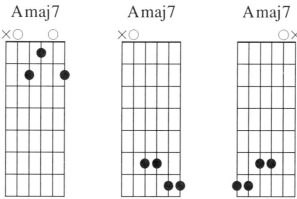

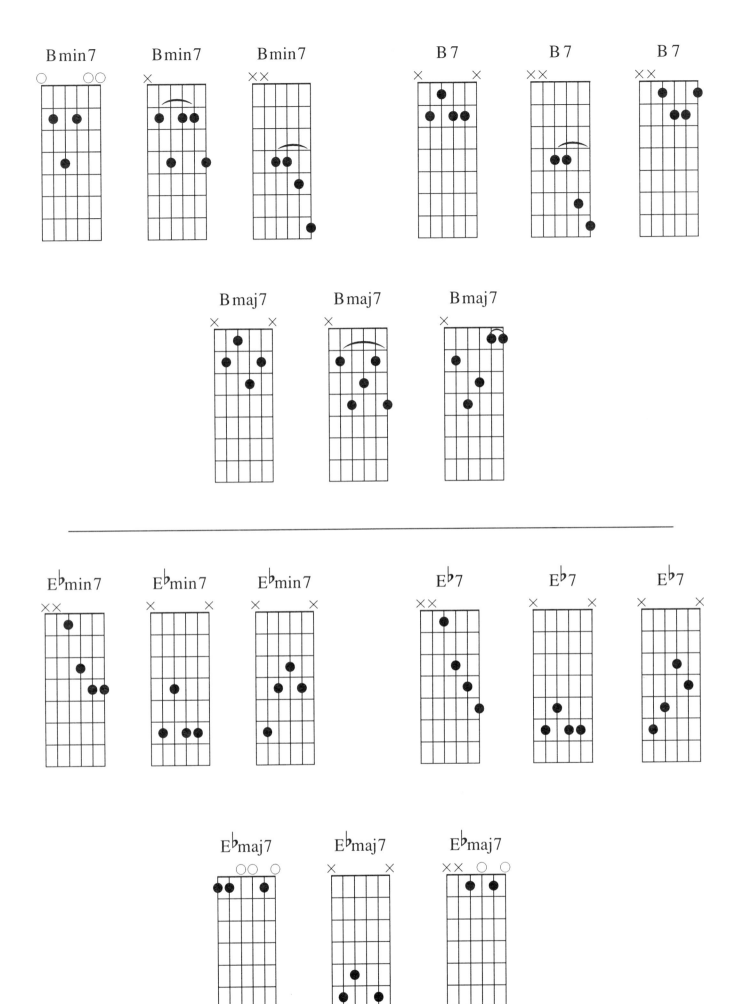

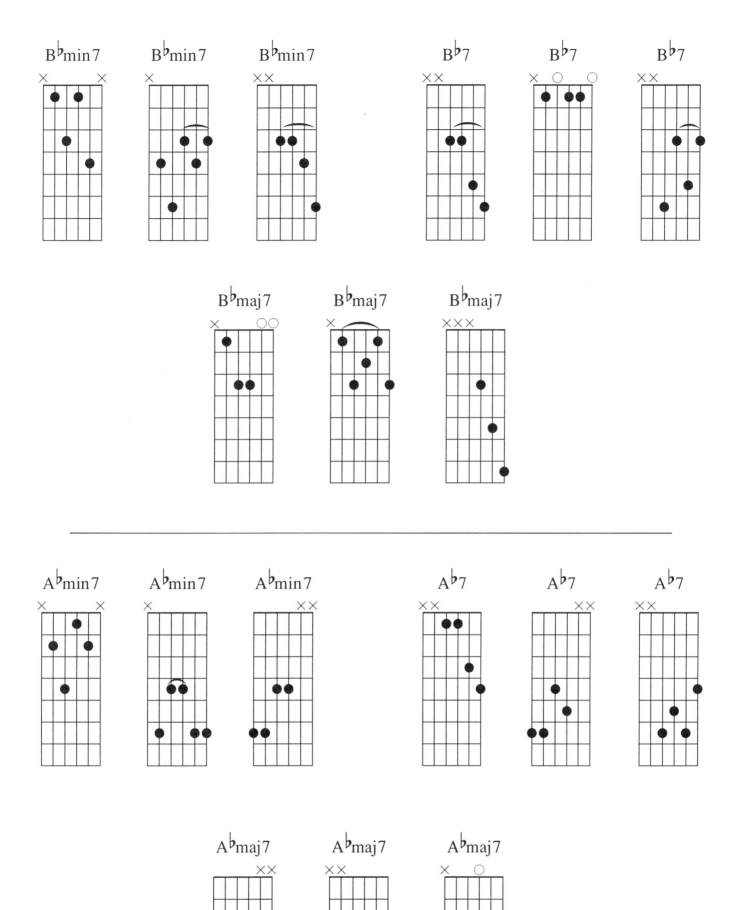

# DADGAD Short – Harmonics and Chords

This *DADGAD Short* presents a combination of harmonic and chord technique. If harmonics are new to you see the section on *Playing Harmonics – Natural and Artificial*. The first two measures are natural harmonics at the twelfth fret followed by full chord strums in measure 3. The chord note changes take place on strings three and four with the other strings ringing open. Though the harmonics in the last measure are natural, play them with the technique often used for artificial harmonics, by using your right-hand index at the twelfth fret harmonic and right-hand thumb to pluck the string.

Jim Goodin (BMI)

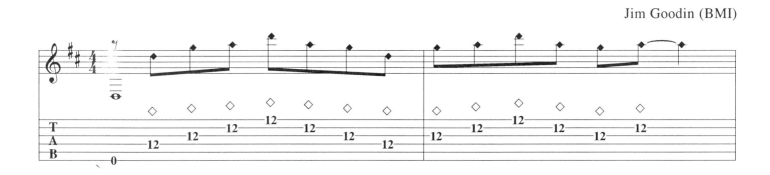

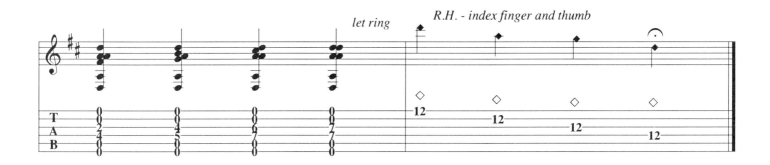

# Evolving the Fretboard III – The Majors

In the third *Evolving the Fretboard* section I return to the major keys to complete the D to D scales ascending chromatically. The scales are A-flat, A, B-flat, B, C, D-flat and D. The scale for D introduced in the first *Evolving* section is repeated here to complete the octave. Where possible I've presented the scales in three octaves.

The pivot-note technique introduced earlier in the book is used in these scales as well. With the scales D-flat, B and F-sharp, there are no open strings to pivot from so these scales are laid out more linearly but still cover multiple positions. I can't over emphasize the importance of being able to move freely about the fretboard. The purpose of all the scale exercises introduced in *DADGAD Encyclopedia* is to cultivate that ability. The freer you become moving about the fretboard of your instrument the more confident as a player you will become. This section completes the twelve major keys. As I've said in each of these sections, do not be concerned with speed as scales can sometimes seduce you into doing. Just concentrate on being fluid and clear as you play through each scale. Remember that the tablature is there to be your flashlight on the path through unfamiliar territory; let it guide you.

*Guitar detail*

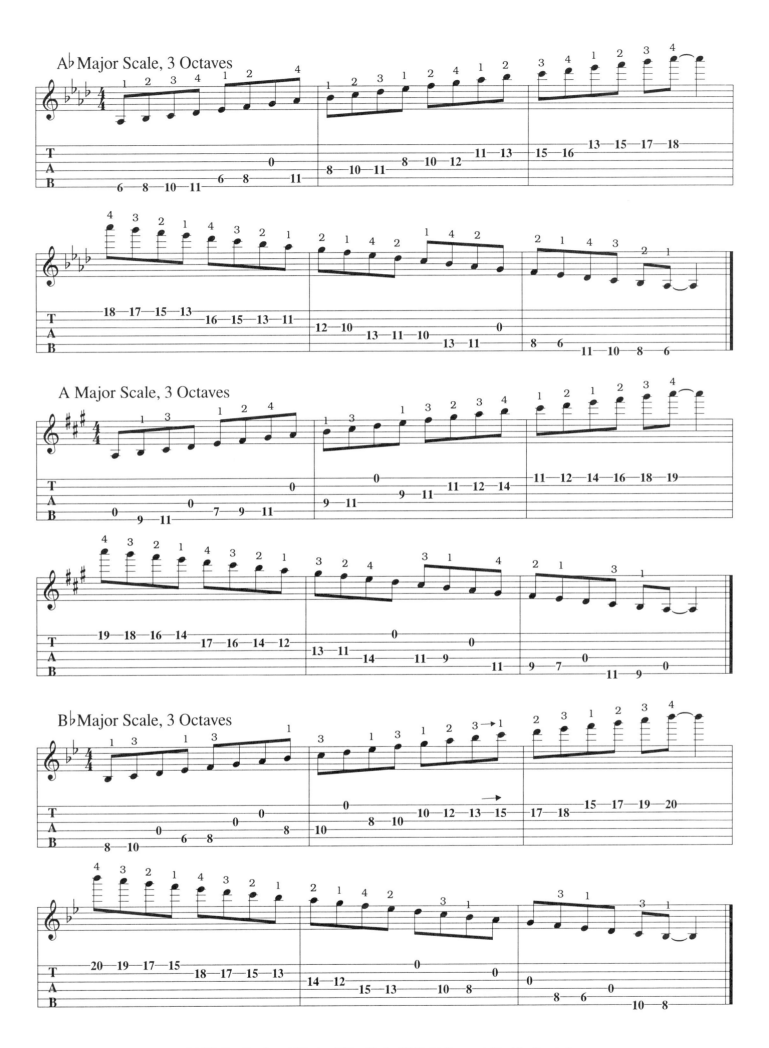

## B♭ Major Scale, 3 Octaves

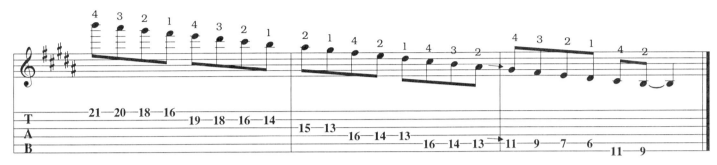

## C Major Scale, 2 Octaves

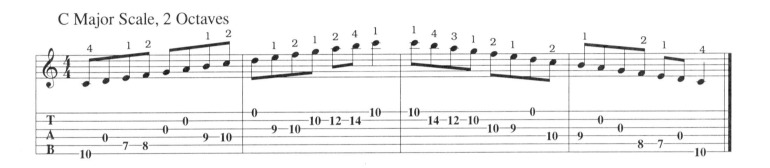

## D♭ Major Scale, 2 Octaves

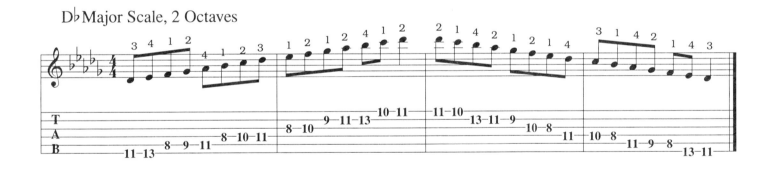

## D Major Scale, 2 Octaves

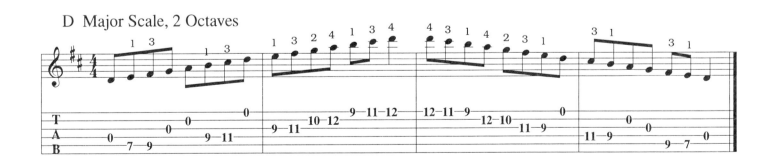

# Playing Harmonics – Natural and Artificial

Harmonics are bell-like tones that enhance the sound of the guitar and when used at just the right places can be the spice in our music. They can be produced naturally and what I mean by naturally is at their physical places where they occur naturally on their given strings, this being the 5th, 7th and 12th fret locations on the fretboard.

With the guitar tuned to DADGAD, lightly place a finger on the 4th D string, not pushing down on the string as you would to fret a note, but placing your finger on the string exactly over the 5th, 7th or 12th frets and then play the string. A bell-like tone will be produced. The octave harmonic at the 12th fret is the easiest one to produce. These at the 5th and 7th frets take some practice, but be persistent and you will get a lovely harp-like sound. If your finger is behind or ahead of the fret, it will not produce the clearest harmonic, so keep at it until you are right over the fret, focusing on your touch as well as the right or left-hand pluck of the string.

Artificial harmonics are produced by fretting a note as if you would play it but instead, with the note fretted by the left hand go up exactly twelve frets to the fretted note's octave. Place your right-hand index finger exactly over that octave fret as if playing a natural harmonic and pluck the string with your thumb or ring finger flesh or nail. If you have properly followed these steps you will be able to produce the harmonic for that fretted note. Using this technique you can play artificial harmonics anywhere on the fretboard as long as you have scale length to play them twelve frets or an octave above the fretted note.

*This illustration shows both natural and artificial harmonics.*

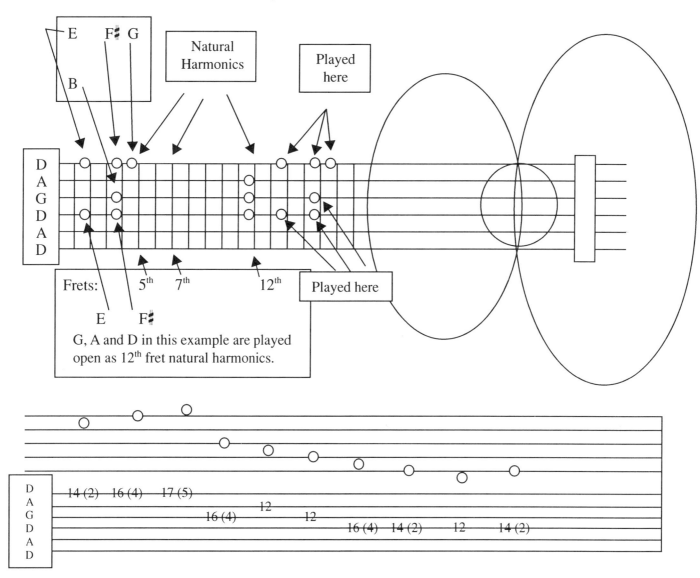

In the notation above, numbers in parenthesis represent the left hand fretted notes and numbers outside the parenthesis are the right-hand, octave-higher artificial harmonic notes. In this example I have noted a partial passage from the ending of my piece "Standing at the Gate." The passage begins on E fretted at the second fret on the first D string. Twelve frets above that E at the 14th fret use the artificial harmonic technique described above using the right-hand index finger and thumbnail to produce the corresponding harmonic. Then fret the F-sharp and G playing the artificial harmonics twelve frets above in the same way. Shift to the third G string and fret B at the 4th fret playing the artificial harmonic twelve frets above at its octave, then play open natural harmonics at the 12th fret for the A on the second and G on the third strings respectively. Next fret the F-sharp on the fourth D string at the 4th fret. Find its artificial harmonic twelve frets above. Come down to the 2nd fret E and follow-through with the same technique. Play an open D-natural 12th fret harmonic on this same D string and come back to the 2nd fret E with it's artificial harmonic to finish the passage. In the actual *Standing at the Gate* notation I end this part of the composition on a chord cluster instead of the harmonic as shown here. I'm indicating a harmonic here as its more pertinent to the concept being illustrated.

Once you are comfortable with the artificial harmonic technique the expressive possibilities it can bring to your music are at your creative whim. Enjoy and ring!

"I liked the stuff you played yesterday — reminded me of the time I lived in England and sat in the Irish pubs drinking really dark beers" – *Joseph, clinic attendee*

*Performing at a GHS String clinic at Sam Ash Music in New Haven, CT*
*Photo by Leslie Hutchison*

# "Quarrel with the Landlady" and "Standing at the Gate"

History tells us that O'Carolan wrote each of his tunes for people he would meet in his travels throughout Ireland, so there must have been a troubled relationship that produced the name of this first piece, "Quarrel with the Landlady." Paradoxically though the music seems far too beautiful to be descriptive of a quarrel. O'Carolan was very influenced by Vivaldi, Corelli and Bach. "Quarrel with the Landlady" echoes these composers to my ears.

Note: The low C notes on the sixth D string in measures 3 and 7, should always be fingered with the thumb which is taboo in some worlds; with the fingering formations I've chosen however, it's the best way to make these passages smooth.

Perform "Quarrel" with a rubato, dreamy feel but still allowing it to flow. Don't worry too much about a strict tempo.

_·_·_·_·_·_·_·_·_

# Standing at the Gate

There was an older woman who lived down the street from us named Rose. I often saw her on nice spring days standing at her gated yard looking out on the world, seemingly dreaming of earlier days.

"Standing at the Gate" is in E minor and makes complete use of the guitar fretboard. At the end of the piece there is a passage of natural and artificial harmonics. See my technique page on *Playing Harmonics* on pages 104 and 105 for help on producing harmonics.

# Quarrel With the Landlady

Turlough O'Carolan
Arranged by Jim Goodin (BMI)

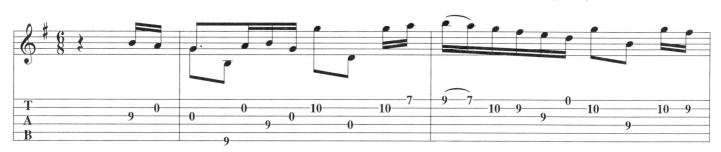

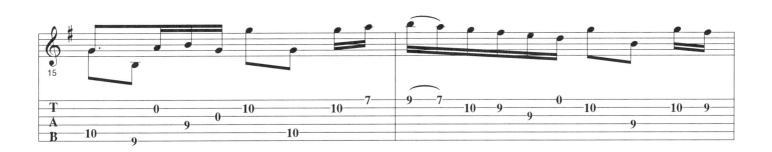

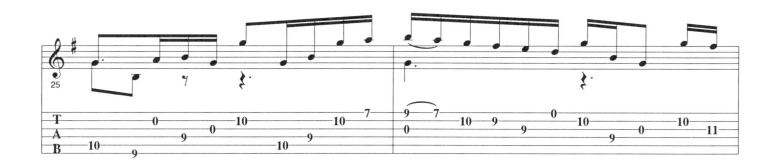

Segue to "Standing at the Gate"

# Standing at the Gate

Jim Goodin (BMI)

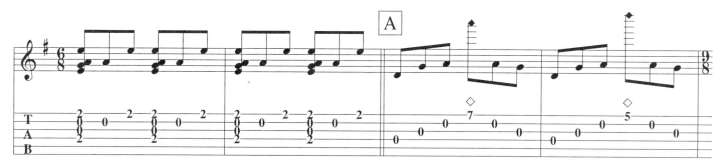

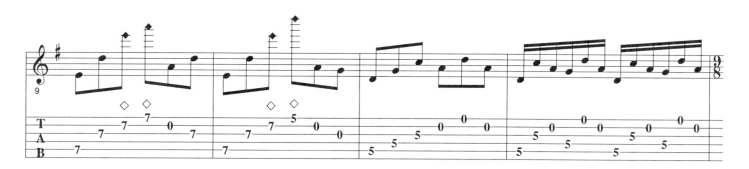

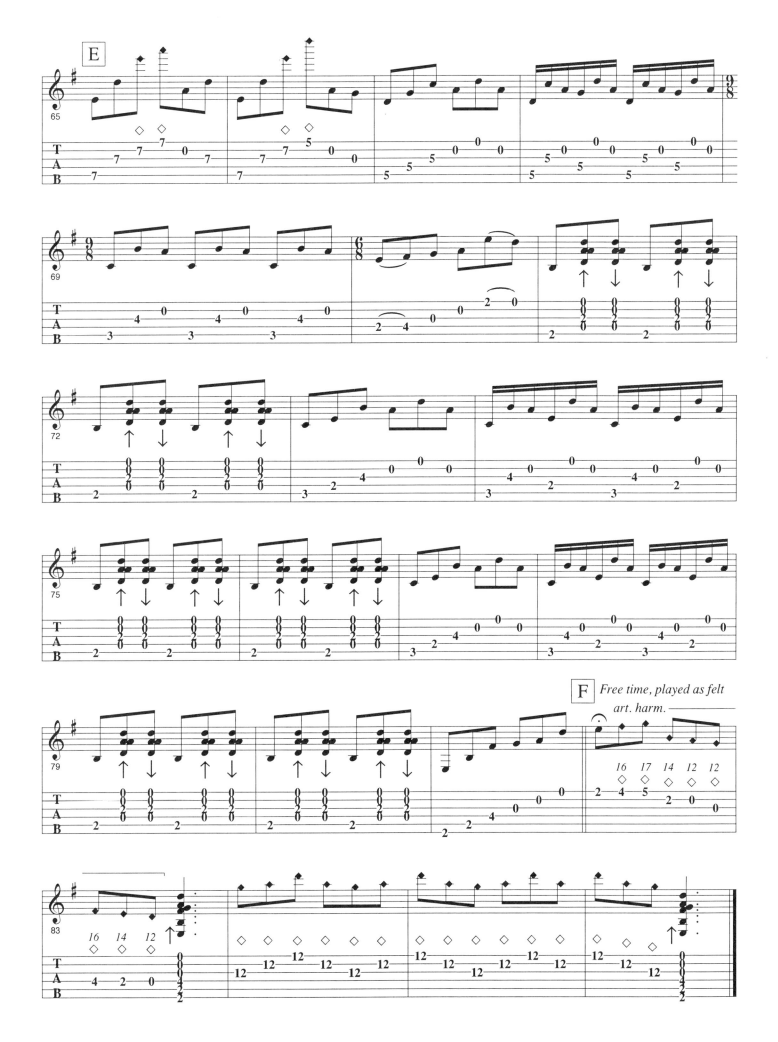

# DADGAD Short – Twelve-Bar Blues in C

For this *DADGAD Short* I composed a twelve bar blues that is great fun to play. I used arppegiated chords throughout this standard I-IV-I-V-IV-I-V-I progression along with adding a flatted seventh on each chord passage to drive and produce the "blues" color. The key center is in C though with any blues there are accidentals, so watch carefully for the B and E notes when they are flatted or naturalized.

Jim Goodin (BMI)

# Arkansas Traveler

*Guitar Detail*

Arkansas is my native state and I've heard various takes on this traditional gem all my life. I wanted to do something with it in a fingerstyle setting and came up with what began as an intro in 6/8 meter. Placing the melody in that meter and feel gave my arrangement the flavor of a Baroque gigue.

The third-string G-sharps will require some mastering. It's possible to play these notes naturalized making them open string notes and still work in this arrangement; the G-sharps however, will give it more of a blues or modal feel. If you can get the sharps the arrangement will take on the gigue flavor I had in mind.

# Arkansas Traveler

Traditional
Arranged by Jim Goodin (BMI)

*Like a gigue,
slowly but building*

B

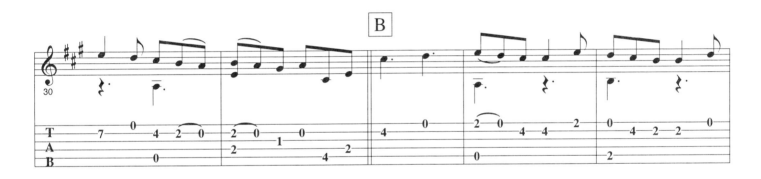

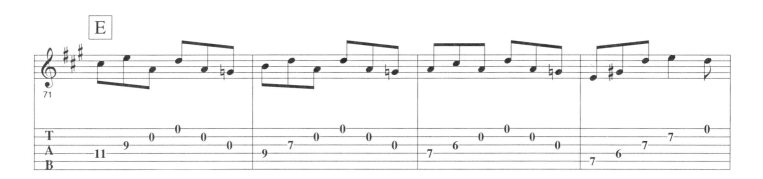

# Chords of Color

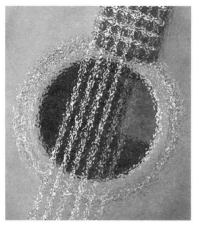

This collection of chord shapes makes use of all fretboard positions through the twelfth fret. These chords continue with the idea introduced in the previous chord section, that of extending the triad by adding a third to create a seventh chord. This time I will make more colorful combinations by adding another interval of a third to make a ninth chord, or a major second to make the triad a sixth chord. Many of the chord shapes included in this section utilize the open voicings of DADGAD and use a minimum number of fretted notes.

If you are a jazz player interested in how the chords you use in standard tuning sound and are noted in DADGAD, this section can give you insight to getting similar colors.

As with all the chord sections in this book I've provided three fingering possibilities for each chord. The concept in doing this is to help you develop greater fretboard confidence. The chords covered in this section are C major 7 (add 9th), C 9th, D minor 11th, D 7th (flat 9th), G minor 6/9, G 9th, A minor 6/9, A 9th, B minor 9th (flat 11th), B 9th, E-flat major 7 (add 9/11), E-flat 9th, C minor 7th (flat 5th), C 7th (flat 5th), E minor 11th and E 11th.

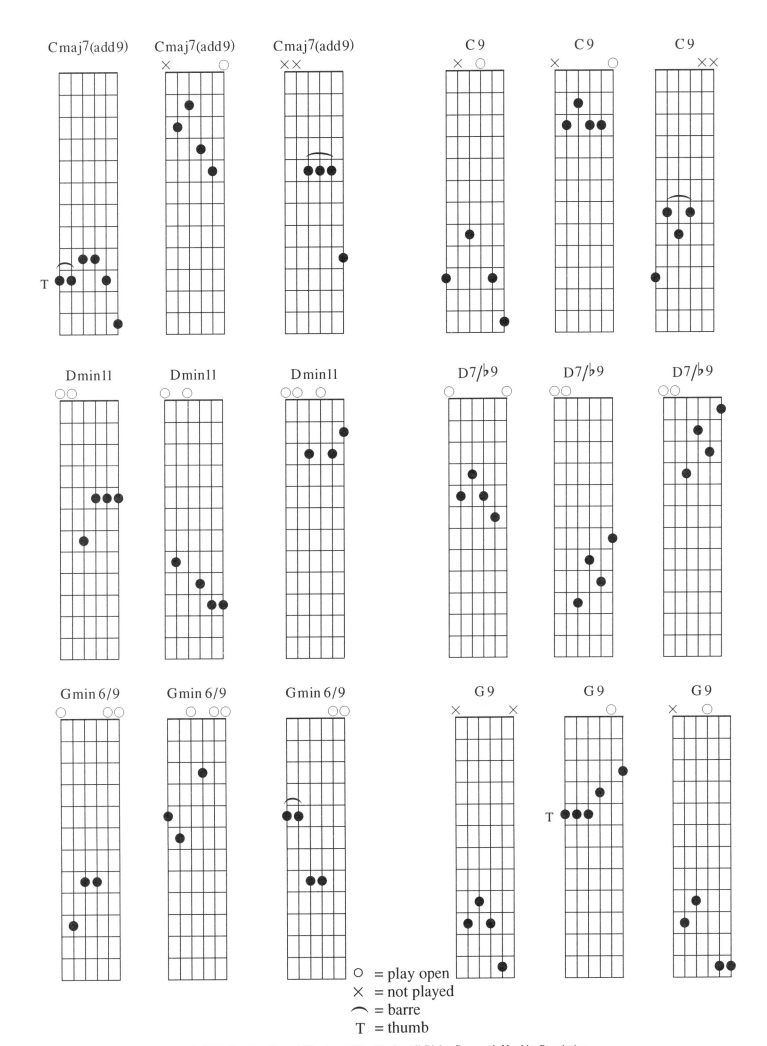

Cmaj7(add9)  Cmaj7(add9)  Cmaj7(add9)  C 9  C 9  C 9

Dmin11  Dmin11  Dmin11  D7/♭9  D7/♭9  D7/♭9

Gmin 6/9  Gmin 6/9  Gmin 6/9  G 9  G 9  G 9

○ = play open
✕ = not played
⌒ = barre
T = thumb

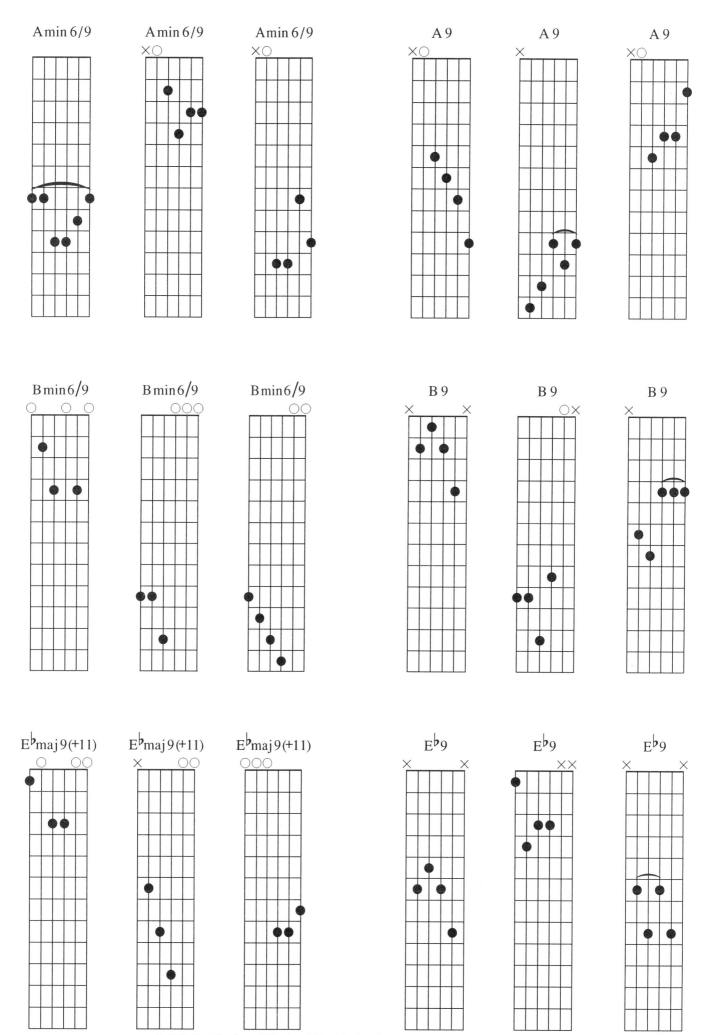

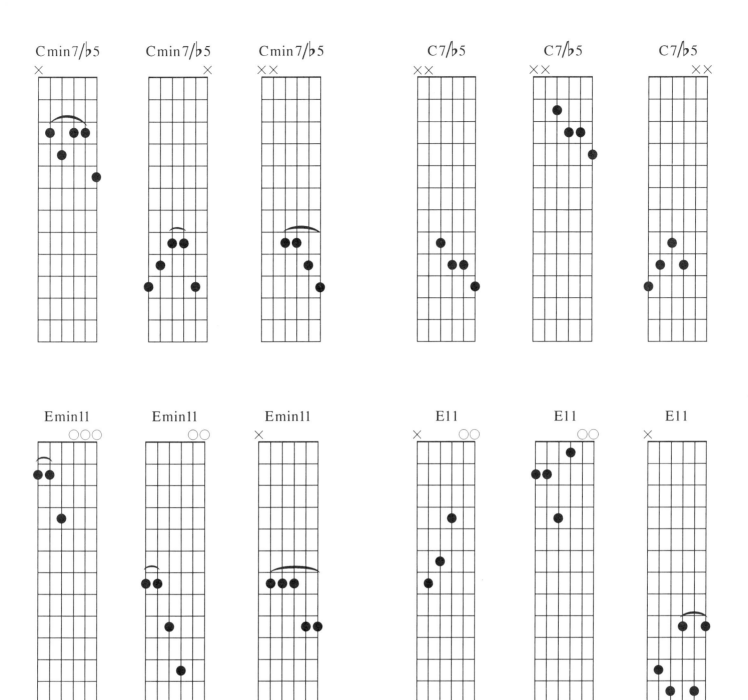

# Evolving the Fretboard IV – The Minors

This section of the *Evolving the Fretboard* series of scale exercises covers the remaining minor keys with their related modes introduced earlier in the book. The keys are A-flat, A, B-flat, B, C, D-flat and a restatement of D, this time in the higher octave. The scales are shown in their three modes, natural, harmonic and melodic.

Where possible I present these scales in three octaves and also use the pivot note concept of shifting note positions that I've discussed throughout the book. I continue to encourage you to play these scales slowly and never really think about getting faster, just think about being fluid and visualizing the entire guitar fretboard. The speed will come subconsciously as the music evolves and as you get more and more comfortable with the fretboard.

*Guitar detail abstract*

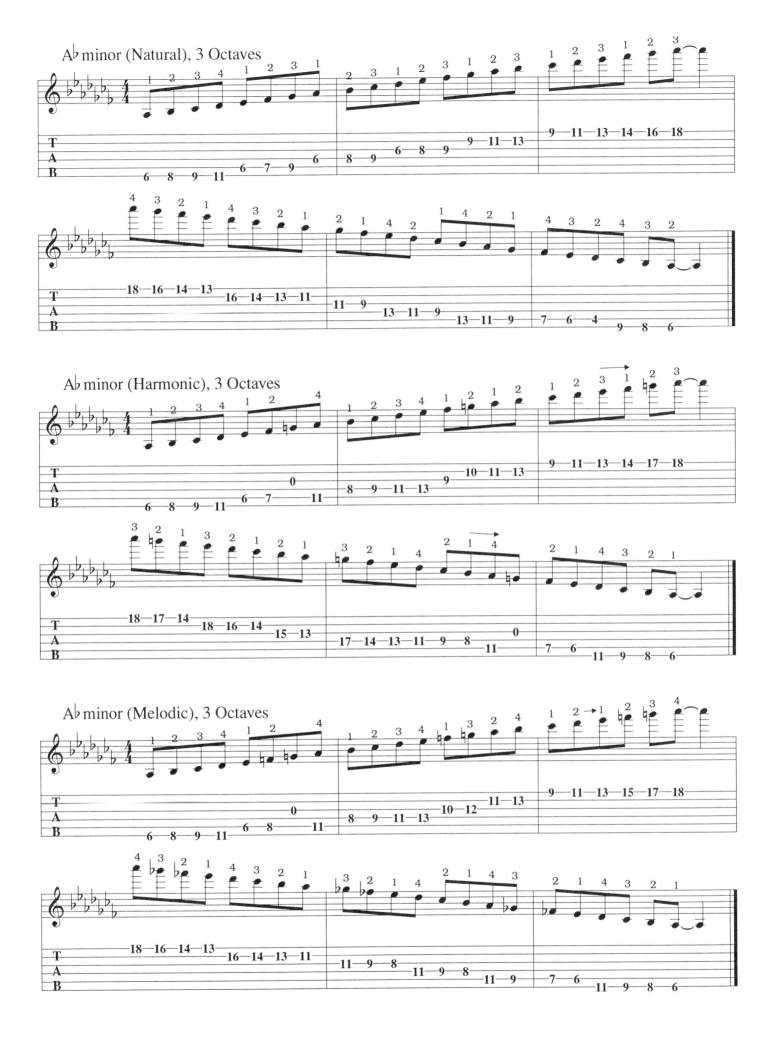

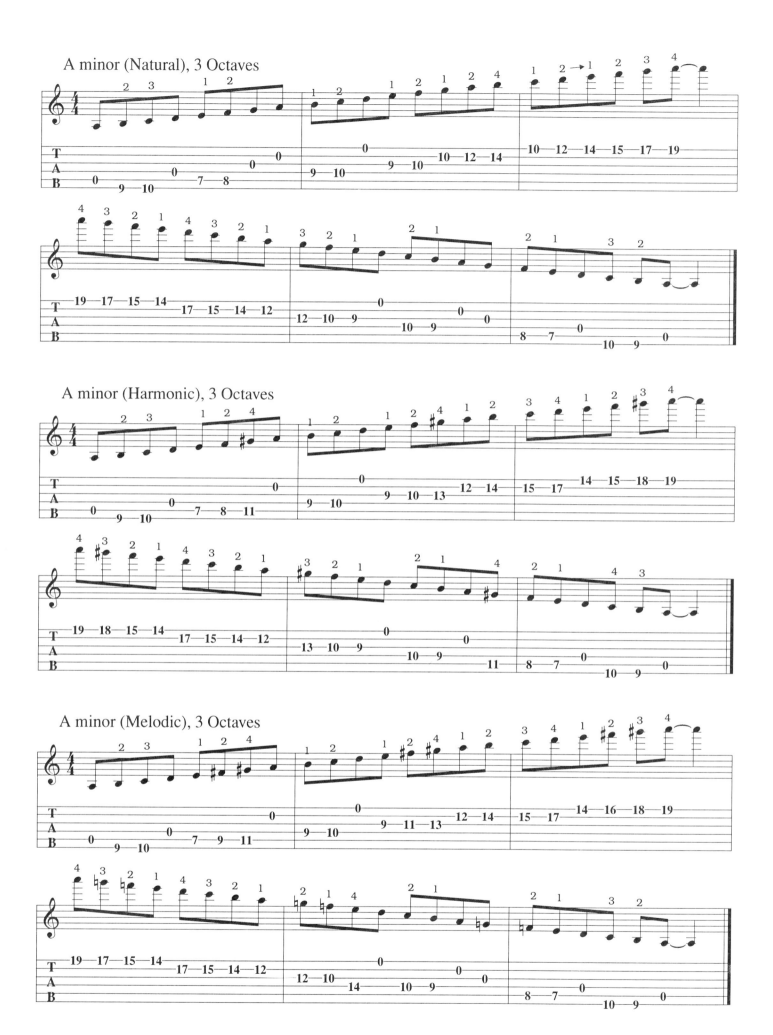

A minor (Natural), 3 Octaves

A minor (Harmonic), 3 Octaves

A minor (Melodic), 3 Octaves

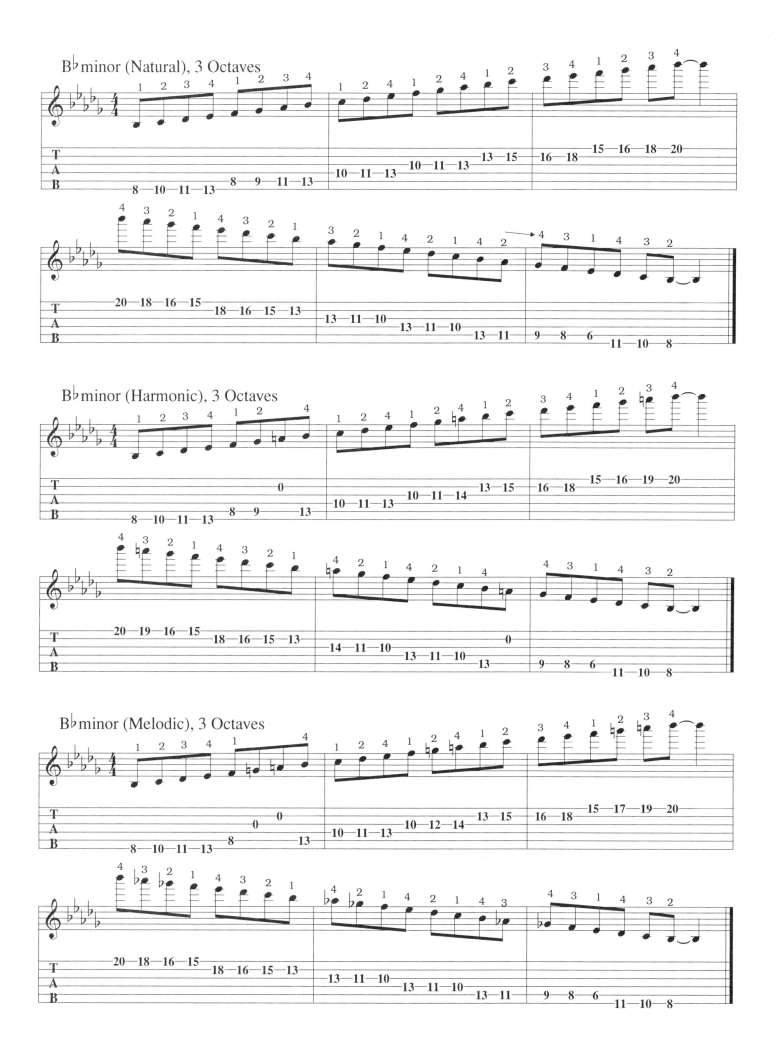

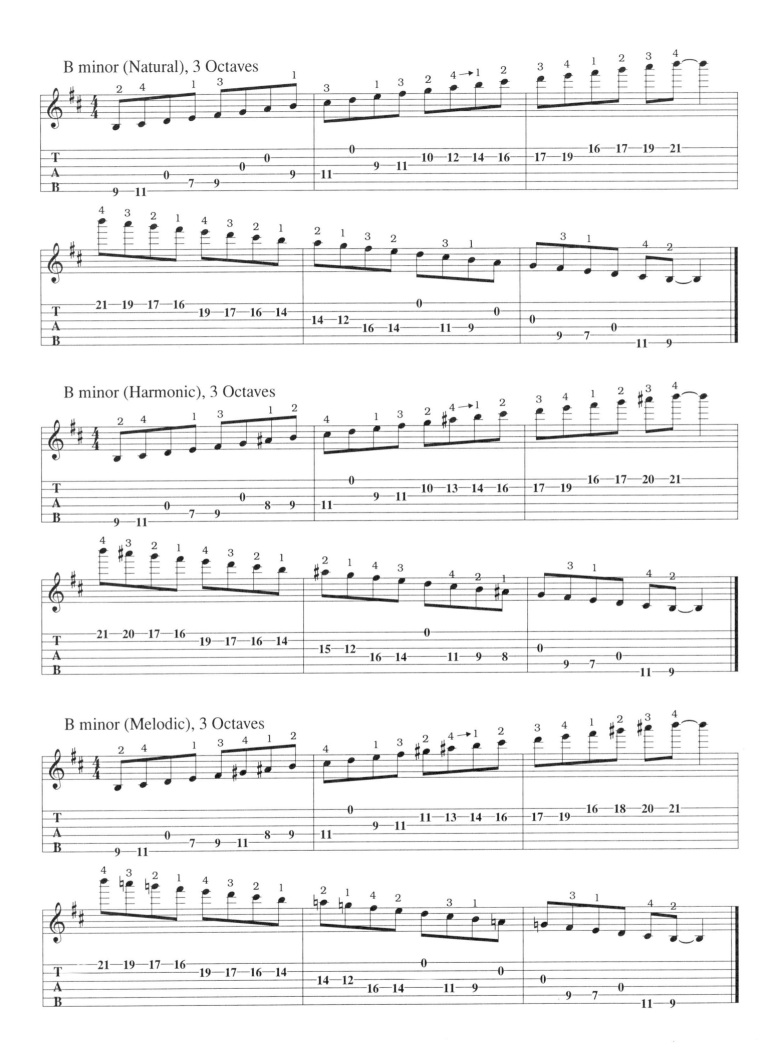

B minor (Natural), 3 Octaves

B minor (Harmonic), 3 Octaves

B minor (Melodic), 3 Octaves

## C minor (Natural), 2 Octaves

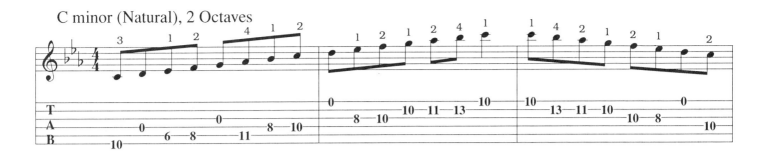

## C minor (Harmonic), 2 Octaves

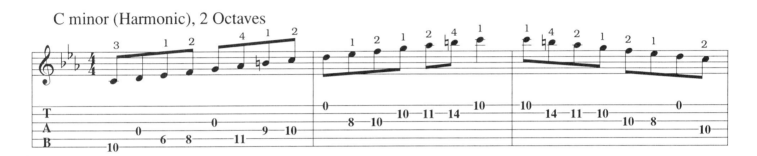

## C minor (Melodic), 2 Octaves

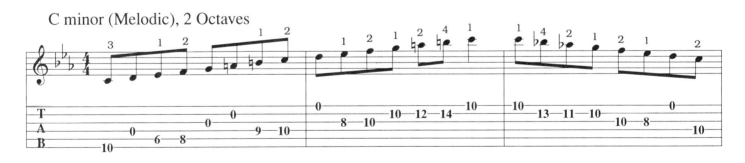

## C♯minor (Natural), 2 Octaves

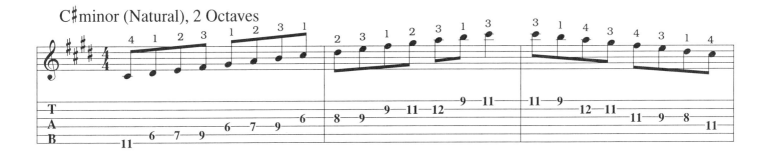

## C♯minor (Harmonic), 2 Octaves

## C♯minor (Melodic), 2 Octaves

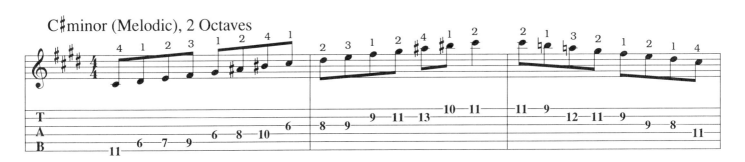

## D minor (Natural), 2 Octaves

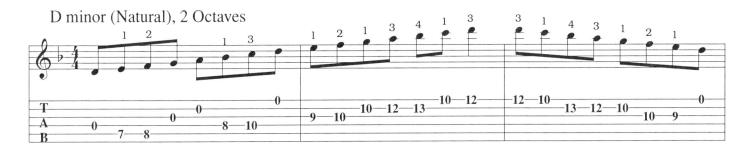

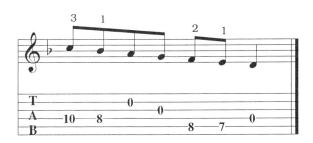

## D minor (Harmonic), 2 Octaves

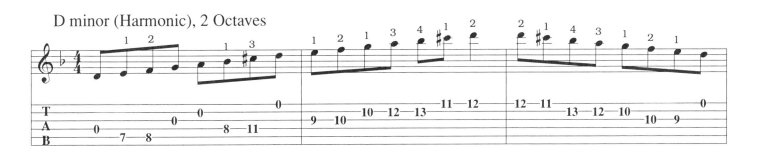

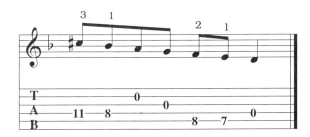

## D minor (Melodic), 2 Octaves

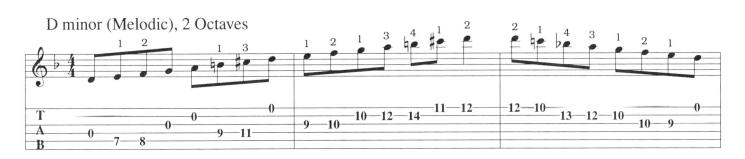

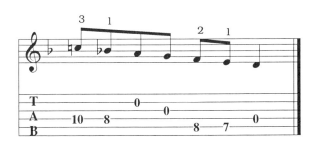

# Farewell to Music

Folk history tells us that this was the final composition of Turlough O'Carolan. The story goes that he knew he was near the end of his life and came to die at the home of the friend who had given him his start with the harp, Elizabeth McDermott Roe. It is said that he had supper with her and then sat down before his harp and played this beautiful piece. Then he went upstairs and went to sleep, passing a few days later.

This piece requires no rush and should be played with sadness, melancholy and a sense of peace.

In measure 19 I noted a fermata, this is a brief pause on the F note as in a last breath before closing. Feel it that way.

*Early morning stillness*

135

# Farewell to Music

Turlough O'Carolan
Arranged by Jim Goodin (BMI)

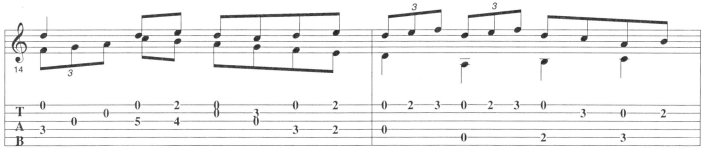

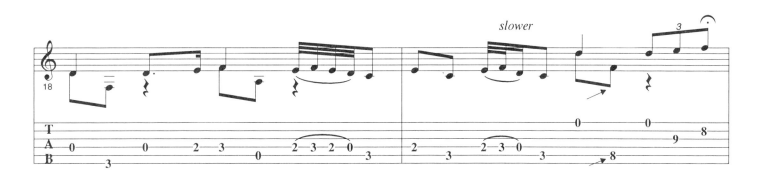

# DADGAD Short – Island Groove

In this *DADGAD Short* I came up with a triplet rhythm feel so that the end result sounds like a calypso or island groove as I suggest in the title. As the feel will take you to the Caribbean, the use of open strings as pivot points in measures 2, 4 and 6 will take you around the fretboard and continue to enhance your technique. Measure 4 offers a challenge with the slide to the high B and a descent through the chord tones to the harmonic but once that is in place, I think you'll find the groove of this *Short* fun to play.

Jim Goodin (BMI)

# Hypnosis

"Hypnosis" was written to contrast with a more rhythmic composition of mine and grew out of the inspiration of compositions like "Two Days Old" and "Magic Farmer," along with a composition by Bill Frisell called "Pendulum."

Once you get the feel for the rhythm of this piece, concentrate on letting the notes ring and stay connected, almost as if one note bleeds into another. Allow the fingerpicking pattern to become ghostly and hypnotic throughout.

*Jim Goodin performing "Hypnosis," as daughter Callie and friend Amy look on.*
*Percussionist Will Romano in the background. Photo by Sharon Romano.*

# Hypnosis

Jim Goodin (BMI)

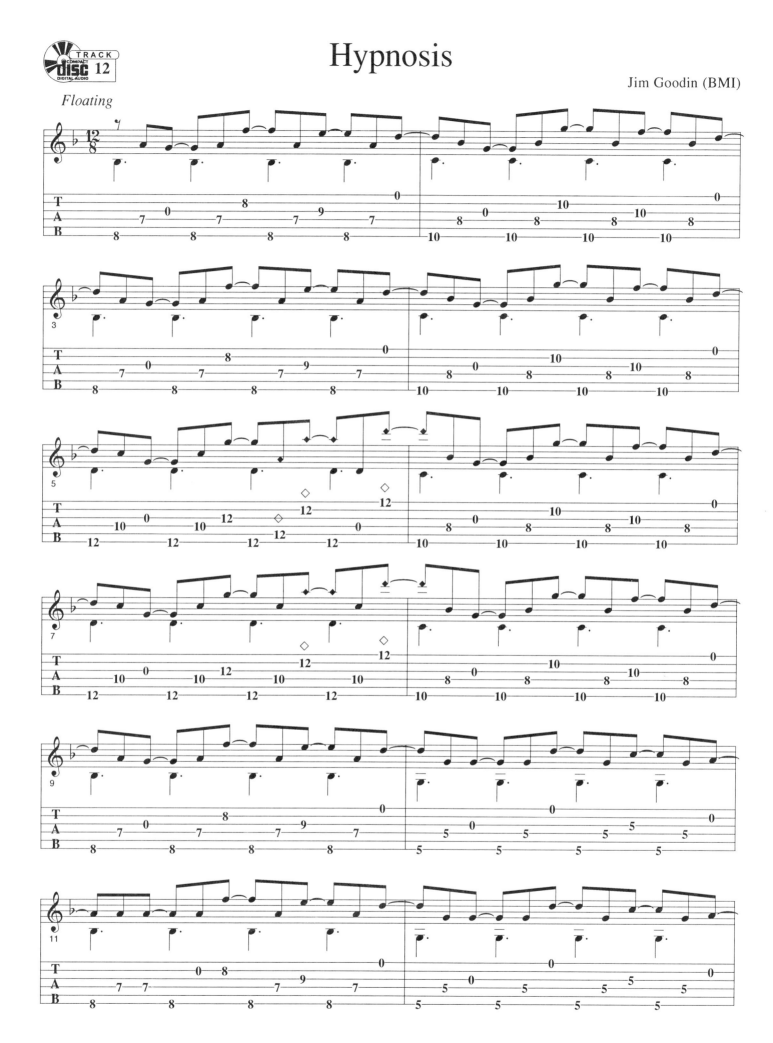

# Apple Mountain Music
**10301 Comanche Rd. NE, Ste 5**
**Albuquerque NM 87111**
**237-2048   www.applemtnmusic.com**

No.: 008814
Customer No.: Lawrence, R
Salesperson: DRF
Date: 27-Feb-10
Time: 11:05 AM

|  | Qty Unit | Price | Extended |
|---|---|---|---|
| tr Stgs Lite | 1.00 ea | 17.95 | 17.95T |
| lopedia | 1.00 ea | 24.95 | 24.95T |
|  | SUBTOTAL | | 42.90 |
|  | GROSS SALES TAX | | 2.84 |
|  | TOTAL | | 45.74 |
|  | VISA | | 45.74 |
|  | CHANGE | | 0.00 |

143

# Experience a Jim Goodin Guitar Workshop

This section of the book includes ideas on technique that I discuss in my clinics and workshops.

There are so many different ways to approach the guitar. It's a wonderful instrument that invites from the most basic to advanced techniques. There is the beginning foundation that nearly everyone I've met experiences on the first introduction, being shown a G chord, C chord and D chord. These three chords allows us to play many popular songs in so various genres of music including country, folk and rock. That beginning is like looking at the outer scheme of a puzzle or matrix. You're shown specific points where to put your fingers to note those chords and then suggested to work on getting comfortable in moving from chord to chord.

The other approach, if you've studied with a teacher who is either classically trained or teaches note reading, is to begin learning small parts of a scale. For example on the high E string, playing open E, then first fret F, then third fret G and back down to F and E.

*Jim recording at Imaginary Road Studios. Photo by Corin Nelsen*

With both of these starting points, while they certainly give a feeling for the instrument, neither reveals the extremely rich potential of the guitar. As a result, some students stay within the confines of the first three frets for their entire guitar experience. One approach I like to take is to slowly introduce ideas like those I've suggested throughout this book to help you move around the entire fretboard and beyond the first few frets.

In a *Jim Goodin Guitar Workshop* if I find my audience is either new to the instrument or has played for some time but not progressed as they would like, I try several ideas to help them break into the realization of the overall fretboard or at least, to the twelfth fret.

As I have discussed a few times in other sections of this book, one approach is to use the guitar's open strings as pivot points that allow the player to change positions quite easily. Once this concept is understood and a comfort level is reached, students find it a very inviting way to advance with the guitar. As I said above, it is like a matrix that serves as a road to find wonderful sounds. The spice is when we discover that a D string third-fret F is also the same pitch at the eighth fret on the A string. If you play a C scale beginning with third fret C on the A string, then play the D string open, then shift up to the seventh fret on the fifth A string to get an E and F at the next fret up. At that point you can play the open G string and being in DADGAD, play the second string open A; next, jump to the ninth fret on the fourth D string and play a B, then one fret up to play the C and complete the scale. This example and the pivot point system will show you is the logic and beauty of the DADGAD guitar fretboard, and once mastered, how fluidly you can move around the instrument. I learned this system early on from Chet Atkins through his columns in *Frets* magazine. This method works marvelously in a tuning like DADGAD but can be applied to standard as well as any other tuning.

In this book's sections on scales I've discussed the utilization of the pivot point method and shown the points in the corresponding tablature for each scale where possible. The scale exercises are a wonderful way to learn to move around the fretboard and gain a sense of fluidity as well as expression in your playing.

In my workshops I also like to introduce what this book is about, I teach players about open tunings and how in many cases like DADGAD its only three strings are altered from standard guitar tuning. I'll often discuss several methods for changing to DADGAD from standard and I have included a section in the book covering three ways to change tuning, the open string, matched frets and harmonic methods.

A workshop with me would also include an opportunity to learn one my pieces with my guidance. We would use a combination of a transcription along with watching my hand positions, breaking the piece into sections. The transcription would include notation and tablature as this book does. If tablature were new to anyone attending, I would spend some time explaining this wonderful tool that facilitates access to our instrument. Really the biggest secret in learning to play in an open tuning like DADGAD is to study a piece that has been tabbed out. It's literally like having a flashlight when you are exploring an unfamiliar trail in the woods at night.

Finally, I hope that a workshop with me would both energize and inspire you in your approach to the guitar, both from hearing and seeing what I do as well as meeting other players at various playing levels. Out of that gathering you'll go home with a different set of thoughts about guitar playing than you came with. I guarantee it! As I mentioned at the start of this section, while we all may experience similar exposure and first efforts with the instrument, the longer you play and immerse yourself in the guitar, the more direct your path will be towards developing your own unique voice. Being around that kind of energy with other players can't help but have a positive effect on your playing.

For more information about a *Jim Goodin Guitar Workshop* please contact me via email at *jimgoodinmusic@gmail.com* or postal mail at *Jim Goodin Guitar Workshop, Wood and Wire Music, 505 9th St., #3L, Brooklyn, NY 11215.*

# Prelude in G Major

I was challenged for this book to provide a broad overview of music including a classical selection. I chose J.S. Bach's "Prelude in G Major" from the *Six Suites for Unaccompanied Cello*. The piece plays well in DADGAD and can be played at any tempo, still offering beautiful sounds and detail.

The main challenge is to get used to the extended left-hand finger positions in the opening measures; but once there, you will be well on your way to playing this piece.

If you have short fingers, placement of a capo at the second fret will facilitate your playing of the piece.

As with all of Bach's music, this prelude is tremendously complex and inventive.

*Guitar Detail*

# Prelude in G Major

J. S. Bach
Arranged by Jim Goodin (BMI)

*Melodic with rubato feeling*

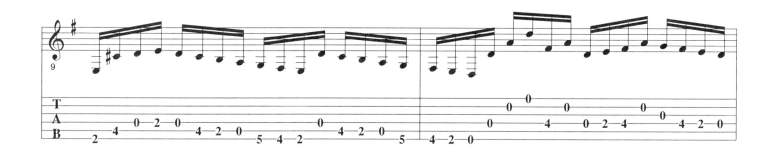

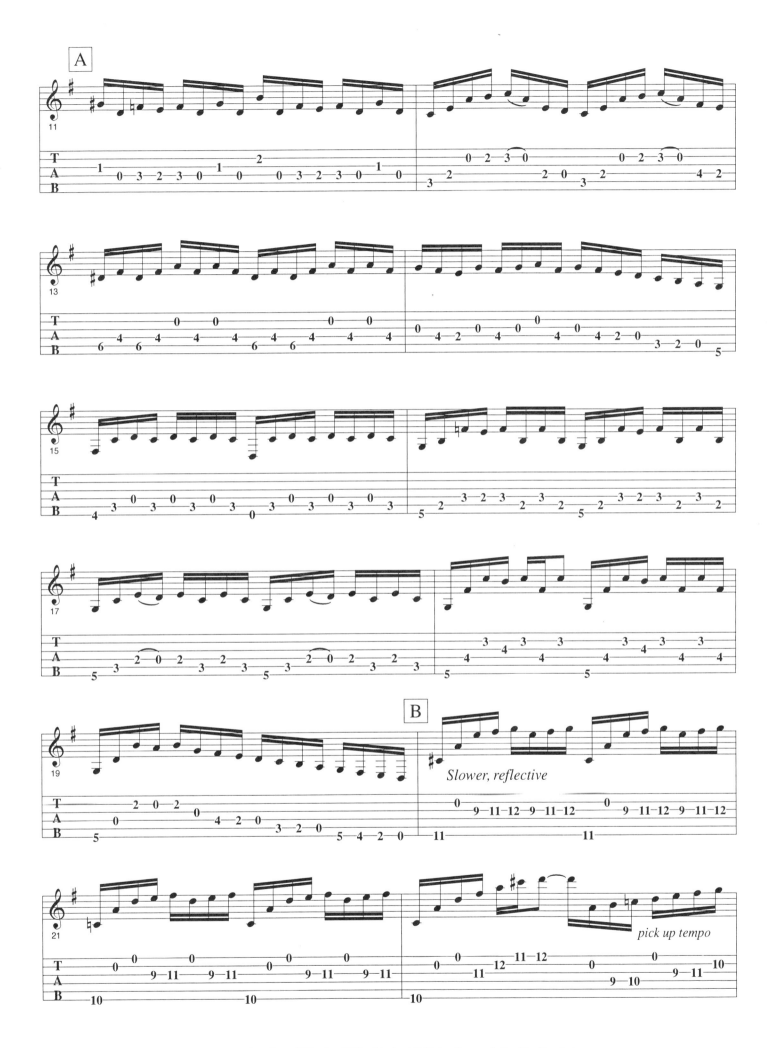

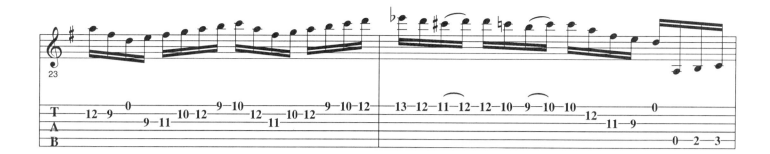

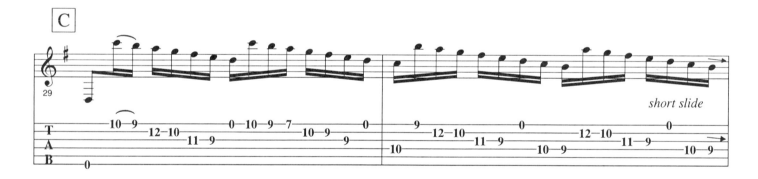

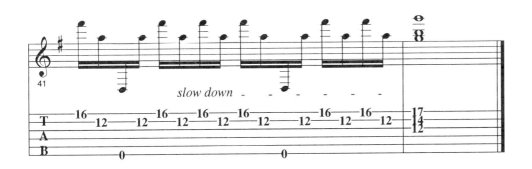

# DADGAD Short – Repeated Pull-Offs, Hammer-Ons and Right-Hand Harmonics

This *DADGAD Short* employs repeated left-hand pull-offs and hammer-ons on the first and third strings and right-hand harmonics on the lower strings to create a counterpart. The harmonics are played with the right-hand index finger at the note's 12th-fret harmonic position with the right-hand thumb plucking the string to sound the note. For more on this technique see my section on *Playing Harmonics*. This kind of two-handed technique can produce fresh new and interesting sounds on the guitar. In several of my compositions, including *The Eagle*, I use this approach to bring another dimension of sound and color to the music. Though the guitar can be melodic and tonal it can also be very percussive. Michael Hedges used this kind of counterpart technique in his moving compositions *Aerial Boundaries* and *Because It's There*.

Jim Goodin (BMI)

LPO = left hand pull-off

RH = right hand harp harmonics

(see text for technique)

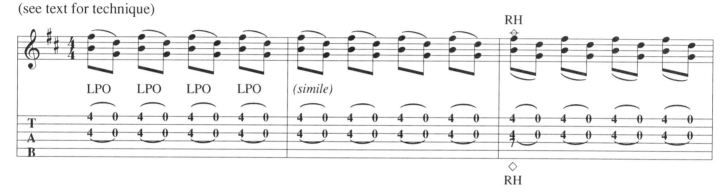

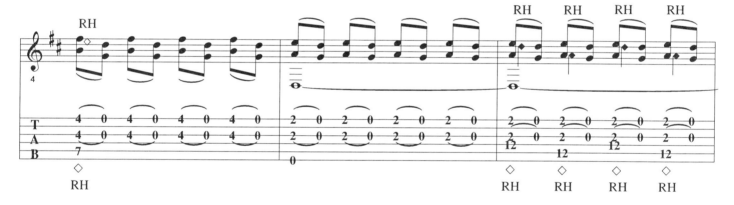

# The Eagle

"The Eagle" was composed initially from an improvisation. As with many of my pieces, it grew from an early inception to a more developed work. This piece is indeed about a soaring eagle and was inspired after seeing the Disney film, *Dinosaurs*, with my children. In the beginning of the movie, you see a soaring birdlike creature carrying the orphaned egg of the starring dinosaur across a huge landscape. This piece conveys that scene and feeling.

"The Eagle" incorporates a range of techniques from straightforward fingerpicking to rhythmic strumming and two-handed tapping. It is probably the most challenging piece in the book, not so much because of technical requirements as for endurance. It is indicative of a great deal of my current writing and feelings about composition and exploring the guitar's full potential.

As opposed to pointing out technical issues, I think it is best to listen to the recording and get an overall feel for the piece; then begin working through it. The notation and tablature is your guide particularly in the tapping section beginning at letter F. The tapping is not terribly hard, just repetitive and really more about stamina. The left hand is doing repeated pull-offs and the right hand taps. I've noted the proper hand-to-note in the notation and tablature. Once you've got this down I think you'll find it's great fun to play.

I like to think that many of these pieces like "The Eagle" are stories. Play this piece as if telling one.

*Working out a transcription. Photo by Ann Jeffrey.*

# The Eagle

Jim Goodin (BMI)

*Moving & Soaring High*

# Sleep My Wee Child

I was working on a project for the World record label *Ellipsis Arts*, which was producing a collection of children's lullabies from around the world. I was asked for something Celtic by the project producer Russell Charno. After I had recorded five pieces to present, I began thinking of a tune called *Give Me Your Hand* by the Scottish harper, Rory dal O'Calahan, a contemporary of O'Carolan. I began to play and improvise with that melody in my head, and thus this piece was born. It is the piece Russell chose for the project. *Sleep My Wee Child* can be found on *Mother Earth Lullaby*, released by *Ellipsis Arts*.

Play it happily with a steady flow, observing the occasional tempo changes as noted.

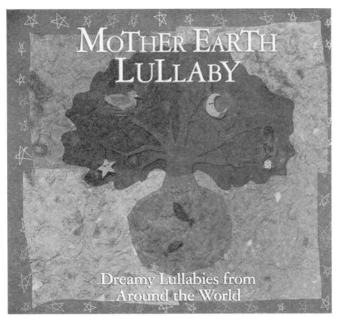

*Cover by Jo E Design. Produced by Russell Charno D.C. Ellipsis Arts*

# Sleep My Wee Child

Jim Goodin (BMI)

*Subtley, dreamy & floating*

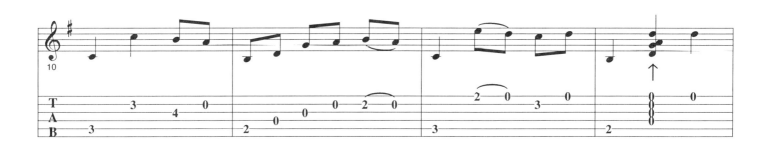

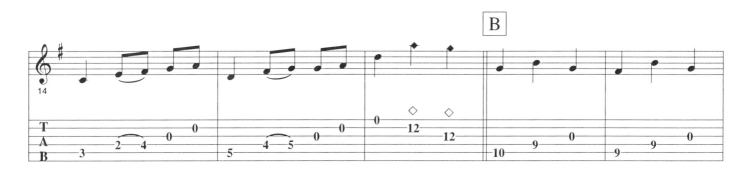

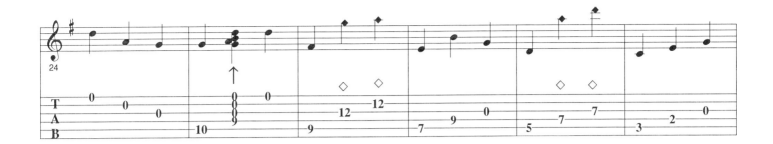

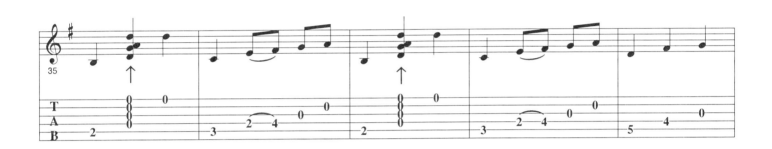

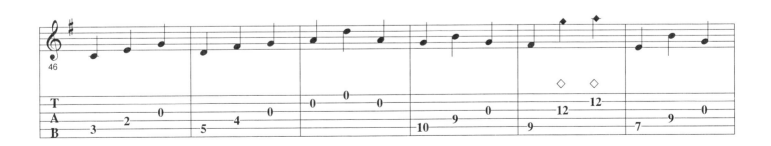

169

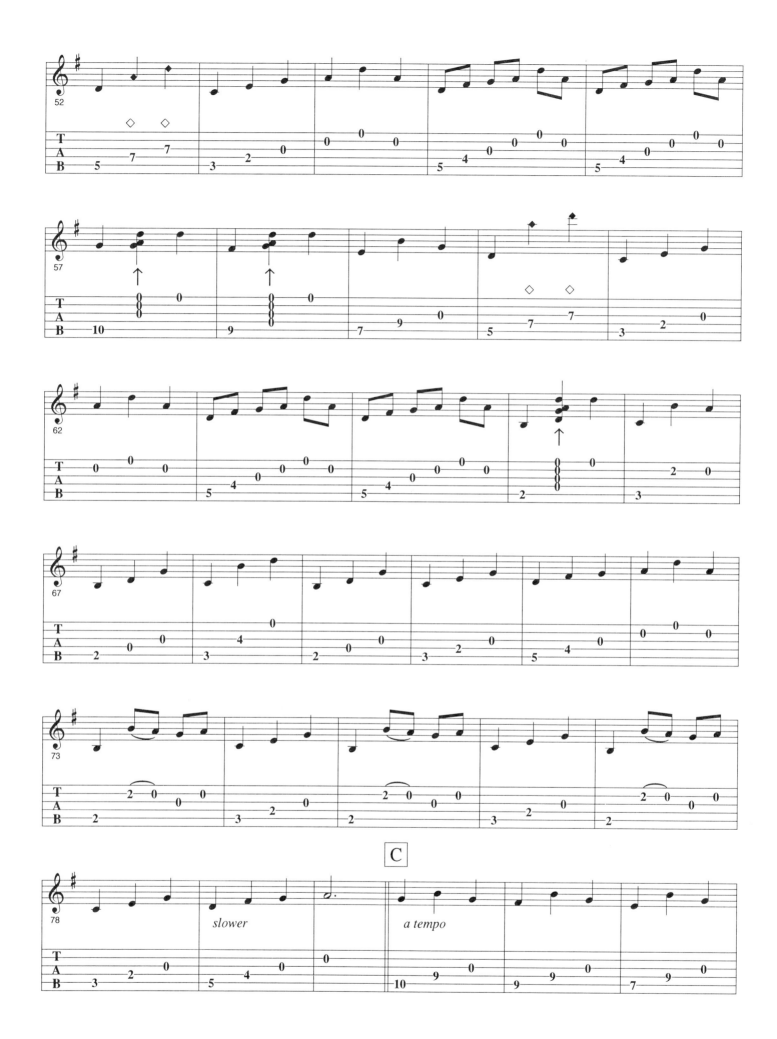

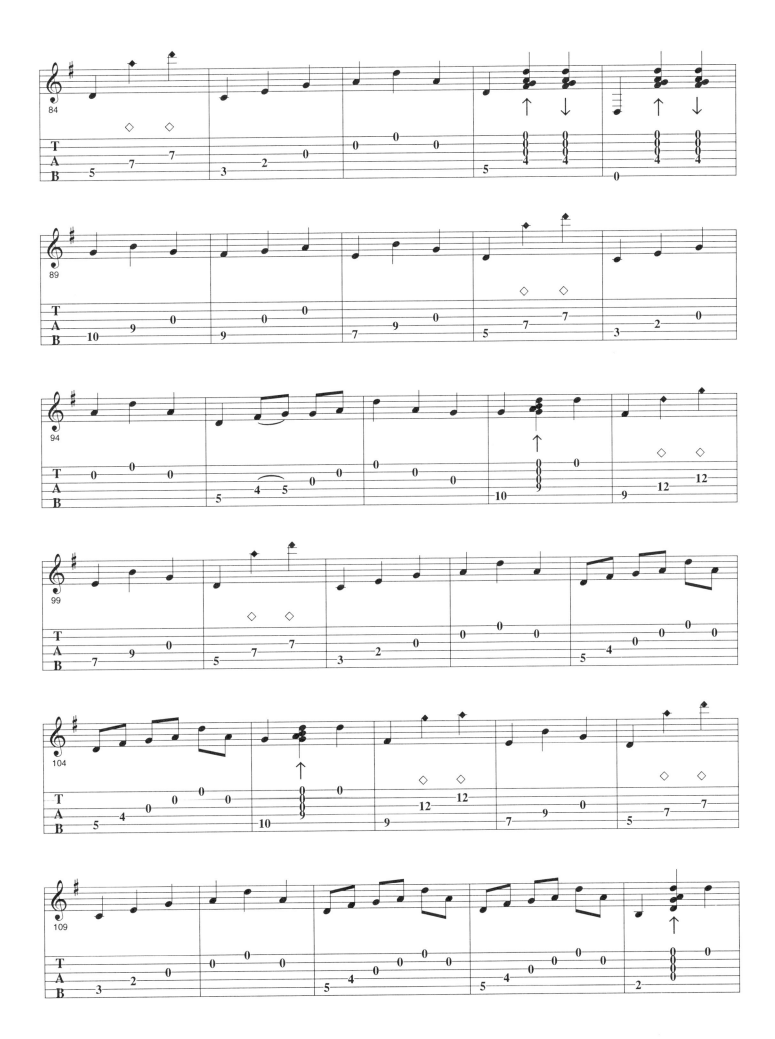

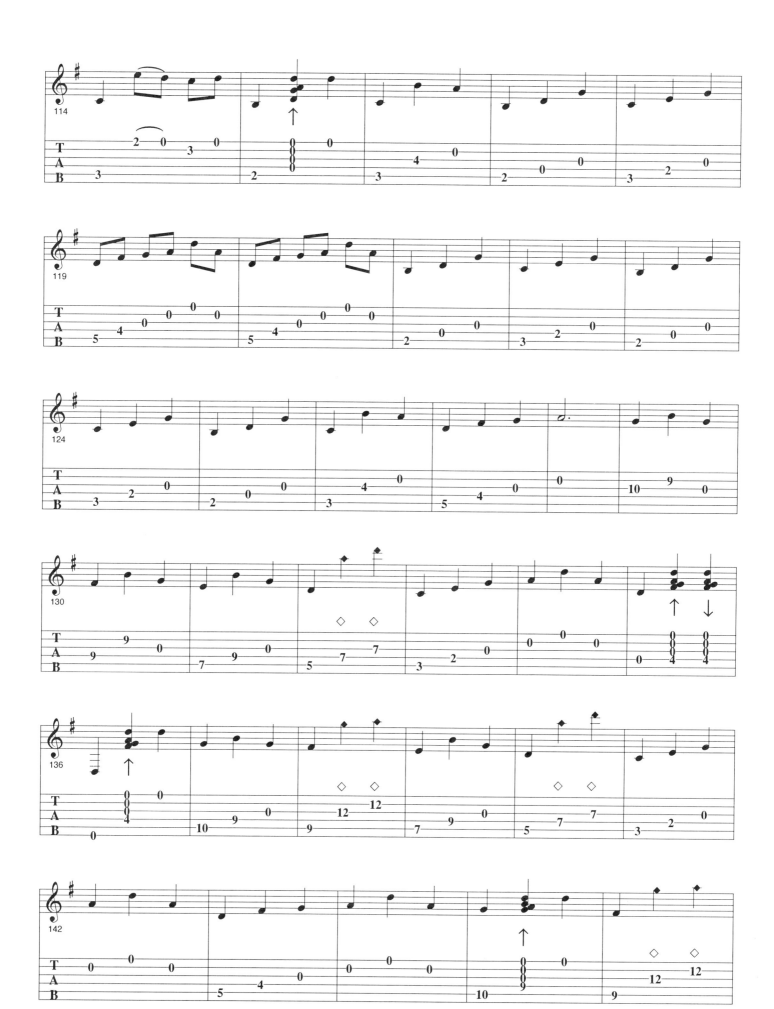

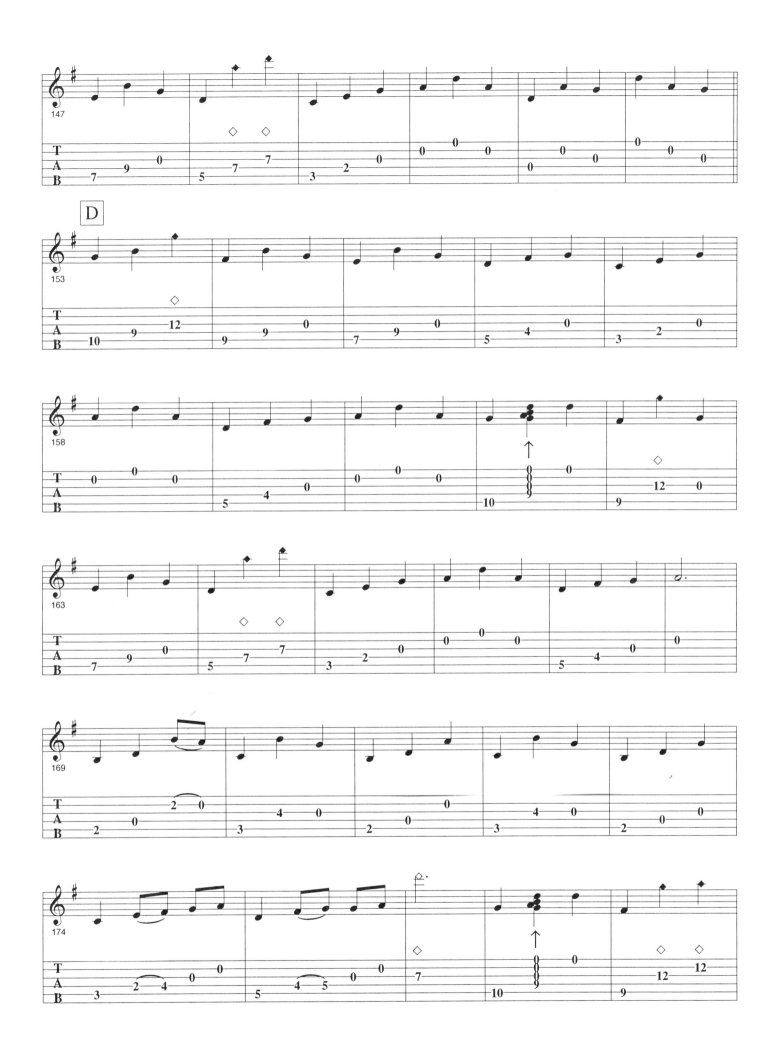

# Suggested Listening

The last several years have brought many wonderful players and music to the guitar scene and particularly in the acoustic fingerstyle genre. I will include here some recordings for suggested listening which have been favorites and inspirations for me. Although this book is about an approach to a particular guitar tuning, I have chosen to include artists who not only work in many guitar tunings and techniques, but in other instrument mediums as well. With the book's focus on DADGAD, think of it not as something unto itself, but more of an extension of the instrument leading to further discovery. That's the way the artists I'm including here approach what they do. As a developing guitarist, it's essential to listen <u>beyond</u> the guitar world though as players we can't help being drawn to what others are doing and creating with the instrument. That said, consider this listing of recordings as exposure to a wider frontier of music.

**Michael Hedges,** *Breakfast in the Field* (Windham Hill). From Michael I gained a whole sense of musical focus for which I will always be grateful. He was an innovator of the instrument but really wanted to be known as a composer first and guitarist second, perhaps third, as he was once quoted, "I'm just a musician, just like you." Give particular attention on this recording to *The Happy Couple*. It's a wonderful and very introspective composition and in many ways started it all for me.

**William Ackerman,** *Past Light* (Windham Hill). Though Will has many wonderful records, this is a favorite of mine. He was the driving force and founder of Windham Hill Records, and many credit him with having begun the renaissance of the acoustic guitar as a solo instrument in recent years. On this recording pay particular attention to the piece *Threes*, featuring Will, Michael Hedges and bassist, Michael Manring.

**Ralph Towner and John Abercrombie,** *Sargasso Sea* (ECM). These are wonderful artists and their collaborative recording documents some stirring musicianship. Towner plays acoustic 12-string and nylon 6-string with Abercrombie on electric 6-string.

**Steve Reich,** *Different Trains* (ECM). One of the great living composers of minimalist music, Reich, has produced a wealth of material. This record features one suite with the Kronos Quartet and another with the eclectic guitarist, Pat Metheny.

**Michael Masley,** *Life in the Vast Lane* (Tonehenge Productions). I first heard Michael perform at Fisherman's Wharf in San Francisco. I met him again at a NAMM show. He composes and performs stirring, visual instrumental music on the *cymbalom*, a multiple course cousin to the hammered dulcimer. Michael plays with ten hammers of his own making that allow him to strike and rub the strings at the same time, producing a wide range of moving textures.

**Richard Leo Johnson,** *Fingertip Ship* (Blue Note). Richard is an amazing composer and guitarist. He is also a friend who has been a constant inspiration since I first heard him in the late 80's. His goal is to take the guitar to uncharted ground, including achieving an almost "unguitar-like" character that bristles with energy.

**Robin Williamson** - Harpist, composer, guitarist, fiddler, citternist and consummate storyteller who could best be described as a modern day bard. He led the legendary *Incredible String Band* during the 60s and 70s and has since been featured in many ensemble and solo projects. His recordings are too numerous to list here but any of them will provide a magical and inspirational listening journey. He recorded two collections of Scottish harp music that I highly recommend. It was also through him that I first learned some of the O'Carolan tunes, such as *Si Beag Si Mhor*.

**Alex de Grassi,** *A Windham Hill Retrospective* (Windham Hill). I chose this Alex de Grassi collection because it covers some wonderful pieces from his excellent early recordings in one setting. My favorites are *Causeway, Window* and *Blood and Jasmine*. *Window* is a fingerstyle tour-de-force paying homage to Leo Kottke. See also the Mel Bay Publications DVD, *Alex de Grassi: In Concert* (MB21457DVD).

**Pierre Bensusan.** Has been called the prince of DADGAD and has done much to increase the tuning's popularity within the open-tuning guitar movement. He is a wonderful player who takes the instrument to new dimensions. Pierre has recorded many CDs; my favorites are his early recordings such as *Musique*, available on *Windham Hill Records*.

**Gerald Trimble**, *First Flight* (Green Linnent). Gerald plays the cittern, which has a mixed lineage; it's related to the mandolin family as well as the Greek and Irish bouzouki. The cittern has five pairs of strings and sounds in the cello range. British luthier, Stephan Sobel is credited with giving birth to the instrument's popularity in recent years. Trimble has made several recordings and has a love for the music of Ireland. He occasionally plays the instrument using a fingerstyle approach and on this CD, "Elizabeth's Air," engenders the spirit of Ireland and speaks of O'Carolan.

**Bill Frisell**, *Is that You?* (Electra Musician). Bill is primarily an electric guitarist but he incorporates an acoustic guitar on many occasions in his recordings. He will often mix accoustic with electric timbres for textural purposes in his vast musical soundscapes. Bill's music is linear and eclectic. It communicates tremendous compositional depth but also a great sense of fun and humor.

**Tuck Andress**, *Reckless Precision* (Windham Hill). Tuck is a great player most often heard in a duo setting with his vocalist wife Patti Cathcart. His energy mixes multiple techniques whether playing solo or in duo with Patti. This solo electric guitar setting features Tuck doing original, popular and standard tunes.

**Martin Carthy**, *Rite of Passage* and *Because It's There*. English guitarist Martin Carthy is a legend both from being one of the main purveyors of the British folk school as well as showcasing the guitar with a great sense of rhythmic fingerstyle technique. On these recordings he is heard in both instrumental and vocal settings. The songs on these two albums are all traditional in nature and content.

**Michael Manring**, *Drastic Measures* (Windham Hill). Solo bassist and composer Michael Manring takes the bass guitar and various versions of that to places that the instrument has rarely seen. Michael often did duet performances with Michael Hedges and in many ways artistically both gentlemen were twin sons of different mothers. This is a wonderful CD showcasing Manring in both ensemble and solo performances. The interpretation of Chick Corea's "500 Miles High" is worth the price of the CD alone. My composition *ManThang\** which I dedicated to Manring's tremendous innovative spirit was inspired by this record.

**Michael Hedges**, *Aerial Boundaries* (Windham Hill). This recording from early in Michael's career has been held up to be the defining record in the acoustic guitar catalog of the last several years. It is indeed a wonderful collection of instrumental music made on the guitar with many unorthodox techniques. The title piece will clearly open your ears and eyes if you have not yet had the experience of this monumental recording. There is a Steve Reich-inspired piece that was developed in part while Michael was a student at Peabody Conservatory and further developed for this recording.

**John Doan**, *Eire – Isle of the Saints* (Hearts of Space). Oregon-based fingerstylist John Doan takes you on a tour of original guitar pieces paying homage to the lives St. Patrick, William Butler Yeats and Turlough O'Carolan. The wonderful music in this recording is brought forth on a custom made 20-string harp guitar. John's instrument has 6 fretted strings, 8 unfretted high treble strings and 7 unfretted sub-bass strings. The album's eleven tracks are enhanced with simple accompaniment of violin, woodwinds, subtle percussion instruments and an occasional synth, but the focus on Doan's rich-sounding harp guitar is never lost.

**Frederic Hand**, *Heart's Song* (MusicMasters). I had the privilege to study with classical guitarist, Frederic Hand when I first moved to New York. He's an incredibly open-minded composer, teacher and musician. This lovely CD captures a very close-to-the-heart feeling, from the intimate beginnings of "Prayer" to the story like and epic pieces, "Catalan Folk Song" and "Willow Mountain." Frederic is also a Mel Bay author.

**William Ackerman**, *Imaginary Roads* (Windham Hill). This is a milestone recording in Will's discography. Though each is a document in and of itself, I think this one remains a definitive stepping in the path. From the opening notes of "The Moment in Which You Must Finally Let Go of the Tether Which Has Held Your Hope Airborne" this record speaks of both exquisitely recorded acoustic guitar and heartfelt feelings of the very nature of the title, yielding a wonderful call and response between Will and pianist Allaudin Mathieu. The recording continues, balancing solo pieces and other ensemble and duo collaborations like the soul stirring "Floyd's Ghost," with pianist Phillip Aaberg. The collection is a wonderfully moving birth of intimacy and the liner notes penned by Will are a narrative gem.

\* On my CDs, *Through the Door*, *Stories My Guitar Told Me* and *Live-Words & Music*.

# About Jim Goodin

Composer/guitarist Jim Goodin's music is a kaleidoscope of influences from Celtic to modern minimalism. With color and tonal sensitivity he writes from the heart, creating music that knows no age or demographic boundaries.

Originally an Arkansas native, Jim lives with his family in New York. He is a published author with *Mel Bay Publications, Inc.*, founder/owner of *Wood and Wire Music*, an endorsing artist for *GHS Strings and Seagull Guitars* and a member of *BMI*.

"I think your music has a real natural ease to it - very relaxed and musical."
- *Woody Mann, guitarist*

*Photo by Paul Bianca*

Jim's solo guitar CDs include **Celtic Journey to the Path, Through the Door, Stories My Guitar Told Me, Live - Words & Music** and the fretless guitar CD, **Found**. Additonal CD or print publications include the **Oasis New Age Sampler**, *Mel Bay Publications'* **Master Anthology of Fingerstyle Guitar Solos, Vol. II** and **DADGAD Encyclopedia**, *Ellipsis Arts* **Mother Earth Lullaby**, **Wood and Wire Music Sampler**, *Chinapaintings'* **Chinapainting** and **Trick of Amethyst**.

Jim Goodin performs as a solo artist and with Daryl Shawn in the acoustic guitar looping duo *Chinapainting*. He occasionally works with the *Language of 3* which he co-founded with guitarist *Matt Richards* and with the *East of Where* duo with percussionist *Will Romano*. Jim also conducts clinics in *Sam Ash Music* stores and presents workshops and guitar seminars nation wide.

Jim is also a photographer and studied at the *Maine Photographic Workshops*. Several of his images are included in this book.

Visit Jim Goodin on-line at **www.jimgoodinmusic.com**.

"Jim Goodin writes with sincerity. His music haunts while it paints beauty. Jim is in no hurry. He perfects his craft and plays in the moment."
- *Rob Lunte, guitarist*

"He is playing out of so many sources that he sounds exactly like himself."
– *Richard Schaub, Ph.D.*

"Inventive and entrancing acoustic guitar works."
- *Thom Duffy,*
*Billboard Magazine*

# Acknowledgements

*My Dad. Photo by Dr. William H. Goodin Jr.*

This book has been six years in making. I would like to thank a host of people. Beginning with my dad, William H. Goodin, Sr., who passed away during my work on this project. My father gave me many things but most importantly, the courage to dream and to pursue those dreams. One of those dreams has been seeing my music walk through wider doors including this publication. I would like to thank William Bay of *Mel Bay Publications, Inc.* for giving me that opportunity both in this book and *Master Anthology of Fingerstyle Guitar Solos, Volume II*. I would like to thank *Mel Bay* music editor Stephen Rekas for much input both on this project and music in general through many email discussions. Additionally, I would like to thank all those on the Mel-Bay staff who contributed their help and expertise in the final production phases of *DADGAD Encyclopedia*.

My love and heartfelt thanks to my wife and occasional editor, Ann Jeffrey, and to our children Jamie and Callie for the patience and support of their husband and father's passion for music.

I wish to give loving thanks to my mother, Marie Thatcher Goodin, who gave me early encouragement and exposure to music through the gift of many lesson experiences with various teachers throughout my youth; and to my sister Elaine and brother Bill for being encouraging siblings over the years.

A special thanks to my fellow artists that I co-promote through my label *Wood and Wire Music*, Joaquin Taboada, Mark S. Greer, Ray Istorico (who deserves special kudos for all the cover art and inspiration over the years), Will Romano, Mario Biferali, Steven Dillon, and Matt Richards.

Thanks to friends, teachers, mentors, fellow musicians, supporters and professional endorsements, Mario Biferali and Fred DiSanto at *Godin Guitarworks*, Dave Cowles and Ben Cole at *GHS Strings*, James Bennett and Sammy Ash at *Sam Ash Music*, Rob Lunte, Richard Schaub, Andy Schmidt, Dr. Scott Hirschman, Jeff Watts, Perran Davis III, Robert Bowen, Richard Leo Johnson, Jason Fiegel at *Music Matters*, John McLure at *Lark in the Morning*, Tom Salvatori, Jim Dickerson, Mark Baldwin (great images and laughs), Fred Hand (who taught me to fall still), Raed El-Khazen, Robert Jones, James "Rip" Westmoreland (for the "Arkansas Traveler" inspiration), and Daryl Shawn for connecting and bringing together *Chinapainting*.

To Russell Charno at *Ellipsis Arts*, special thanks for including my piece, "Sleep My Wee Child," on the *Mother Earth Lullaby* CD and for the permission to include the transcription and a second recording in *DADGAD Encyclopedia*.

The process of making the accompanying CD led me to *Imaginary Road Studios*, creative workspace of *Windham Hill Records* legendary founder, William Ackerman. Words cannot express my feelings about working on the companion recording for this book at *Imaginary Road*, but here's a very special thank you to Will and his supportive engineers, Corin Nelsen and Bill Esses, for the opportunity that made this recording an absolute joy to do. To his administrative aide Virginia Andrews, special thanks for all the support, arrangements and directions in getting me to *Imaginary Road*.

Finally, to all of you who purchase this book, thank you and I hope it brings insight, inspiration and new ideas to help further your path of discovery with the guitar.

*Frenchman's Bay, Bar Harbor, Maine*

# The Making of the *DADGAD Encyclopedia* CD

The companion CD for this book was recorded during three sessions at *Imaginary Road Studios* in Windham County, Vermont. *Imaginary Road* is owned and operated by composer/guitarist/producer, William Ackerman who pioneered major changes in the music industry and single-handedly carved a niche for his own music through his brainchild *Windham Hill Records*. In turn the label brought to light the music of many wonderful artists including Michael Hedges, Shadowfax, Liz Story, George Winston and Alex de Grassi. As a solo artist, Will's introspective guitar creations have helped pave the way for many players including myself. His composition *The Bricklayer's Beautiful Daughter* has become a standard in the fingerstyle repertoire.

*On the road to Imaginary Road.*

Producing this CD through three seasons of southern Vermont serene quiet in the workspace of one of my most important influences made this record a joy to produce. The fifteen tracks were captured predominantly in one or two takes during August and November 2003 and mastered in March 2004. The tracking sessions were expertly handled by Bill Esses and final mastering caringly delivered by Corin Nelsen.

The flow of the music on this recording is laid out with the player in mind, with the pieces

*Corin Nelsen at the helm.*

progressively becoming more challenging as they follow the order of the book. The first piece of music on the CD, "Passage (A Simple Study)" was written as an accessible introduction to DADGAD tuning. The ending track "Sleep My Wee Child," is not necessarily the most difficult but was chosen to end the book and the CD on a positive and aesthetically pleasing note. I have strived to be accurate in my notation and performance notes, but do consider the value of listening to the CD as you work through this book. The recording will provide a feel for tempo, phrasing and style in my approach to the music as well as DADGAD tuning.

My mid-eighties Lowden L27F mini-jumbo guitar used throughout the making of this CD was captured with a matched pair of Neumann KM184 cardioid-pattern microphones placed in a body/neck arrangement. The microphone preamps were custom built by Jim Hemingway. There are only 3-4 of these pre-amps in the world and *Imaginary*

*Road* has two. The microphone preamp output was fed directly into an Apogee Rosetta AD converter which interfaced directly with a *ProTools* hard disk system. The recording was done in 24-bit precision. ProTools plug-ins used were Sony Oxford EQs and ReverbOne reverbs.

*"Sleep My Wee Child" about to be recorded.*

My most memorable recollection in producing this CD was arriving to record in an environment that contrasted so vividly with New York studio where I had originally planned to record this project. On a whim following preliminary email exchanges with Will, I asked about the possibility of recording the CD at *Imaginary Road*. He welcomed me there for the August session shortly thereafter. Arriving at the openness of *Imaginary Road,* I immediately knew I was in a very special place. Will, Bill, Corin and Virginia were incredibly positive and accommodating throughout the sessions. For that I want to say a very special thanks.

*Vermont-Early Winter Landscape*

182

# A Note about the Photographs

In addition to the several performance pictures in *DADGAD Encyclopedia* I've included other photographs that have significant ties to my musical journey. I pursued photography rather seriously at one point and still make many pictures. Whether visual or musical compositions, I feel both contribute strongly to each other. The photographs not credited were made by me. Subject matter for those images include the landscapes of Scotland, Vermont, Maine and a series of guitar details.

I wish to thank several dear people for the credited photographs:

Paul Bianca, neighbor and consummate artist in many mediums, for the rooftop photographs and *Through the Door* illustration. Sharon Romano, photographer and wife of percussionist Will Romano, for the wonderful street fair performance moments she photographed. Matt Richards, friend and co-partner/founder in the *Language of 3*, for documenting me at a show.

I am not certain who took the pictures of me performing for my daughter's class, but I suspect it was one of her teachers, Kate Keim or Bertelie Jules. *Imaginary Road* engineer Corin Nelsen visually captured me in the recording process in addition to the fine audio recording he did. Leslie Hutchison, photographer and friend, for the New Haven clinic photograph.

My brother Bill photographed my dad and me in the poignant image introducing the "Acknowledgements" section. My dad was in the last days of his life making this photograph a hard moment to experience, but it is an image I am very grateful to have. My wife Ann for spur-of-the-moment photographs throughout. My son Jamie and friend Lucio Westmoreland for capturing the very first ever *Chinapainting* performance.

Will Ackerman provided additional expertise digitally enhancing the Vermont road and landscape, recording session photographs and the photograph of my father. I sincerely wish to thank him for his assistance and input.

There has been much expressed of my musical influences throughout the book and I wish to mention photographers who equally guided me through their instruction and influence: Eugene Richards, Dick Durrance II and Fred Wilson. All wonderful artists in their own right and people I feel very fortunate to have had the pleasure of knowing and learning from.

# Closing Thoughts

You are well on your way on a new journey in your guitar playing and musicianship. With focusing on DADGAD, I have shown you the many possibilities that learning an alternate tuning can offer. None of these ideas has in any way been meant to put down or detract from standard guitar tuning, which certainly produces worlds of fine music by many outstanding players. I hope this new knowledge of open tuning techniques combined with what you as players already know in standard tuning will bring your playing and sense of style and musical identity to another level of maturity and artistry.

The concepts I have written about in *DADGAD Encyclopedia* are not limited to DADGAD tuning alone. They can be used to relate to other alternate tunings you will encounter as you explore the many resources open to you as a musician, as well as to tunings you will create yourself as you turn the tuning machines.

Remember that the path of study and play with the guitar and music is not about the amount of time you've spent playing the guitar, but purely about inspiration and developing your own personal vision and identity.

If you have questions or comments about anything covered in this book please feel free to contact me via email at *jimgoodinmusic@gmail.com* or postal mail at *Jim Goodin, Wood and Wire Music, 505 9th St., #3L, Brooklyn, NY 11215.*

*Jim Goodin*

*Music and the instrument. Photo by Paul Bianca.*